# THE ART OF SMOKING

## Mastering Smoke, Fire & Flavor Across Cultures

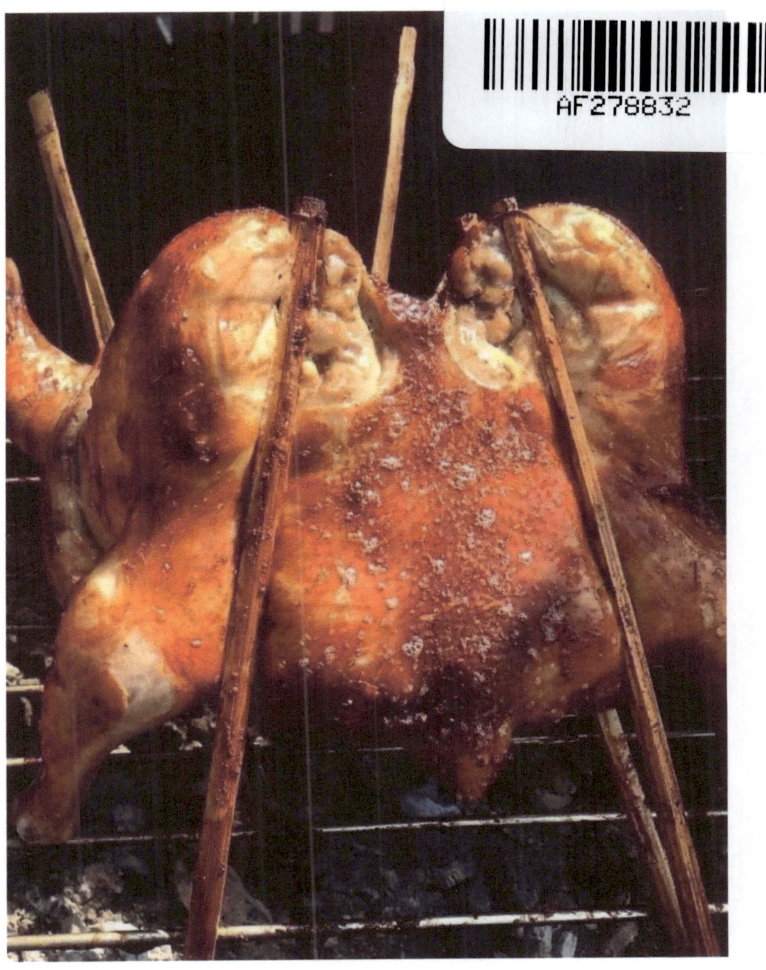

## By Alessandro Asante

# ABOUT THE COVER

*The front cover features a spatchcocked (butterflied)*
*chicken roasting slowly over open coals —*
*a daily ritual at a small street stand in a*
*Bangkok suburb.*

*Before dawn, the vendor and her team light the*
*fire and begin the patient process of slow cooking.*
*By midmorning, the chickens are perfectly smoked,*
*quickly sold, and their workday quietly ends.*

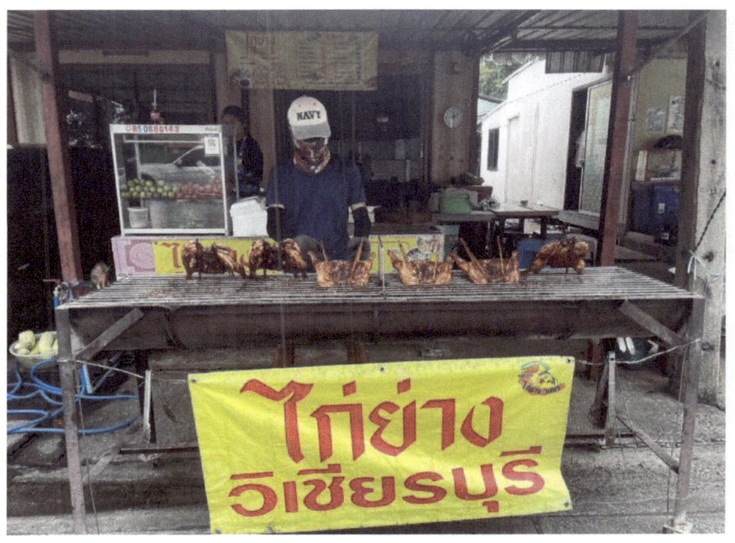


## Gai Yang Wichian Buri (ไก่ย่างวิเชียรบุรี)

*In a quiet corner of Min Buri, this stall carries the name of a regional Thai classic. Each day begins before dawn, as the owner oversees her small team while her cook tends the coals with calm precision. Their early-morning fires and loyal following keep alive the flavors of Wichian Buri, where patience and smoke are part of the recipe.*

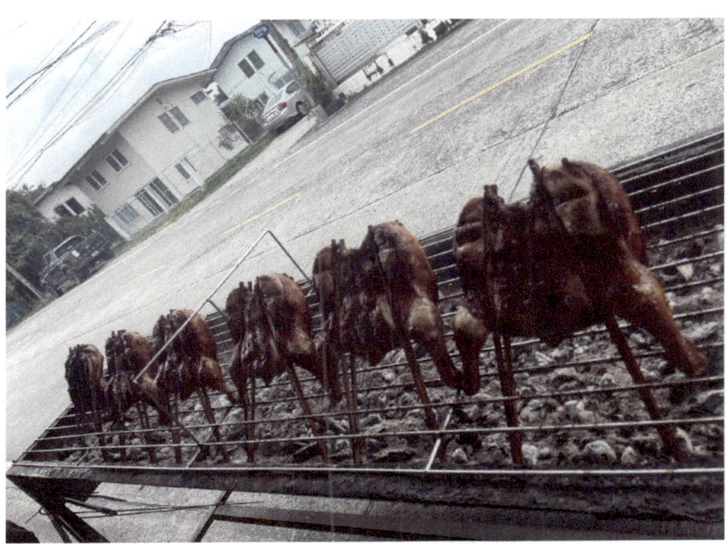

# THE ART OF SMOKING

*Mastering Smoke, Fire & Flavor Across Cultures*

By

Alessandro Asante

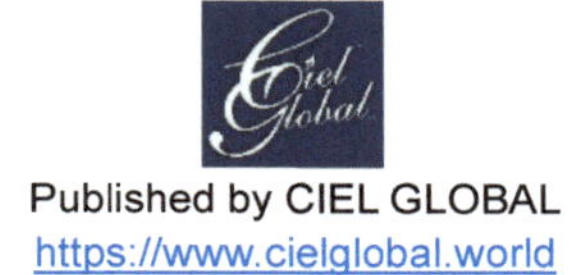

Published by CIEL GLOBAL
https://www.cielglobal.world

# ABOUT THE AUTHOR

## Alessandro Asante

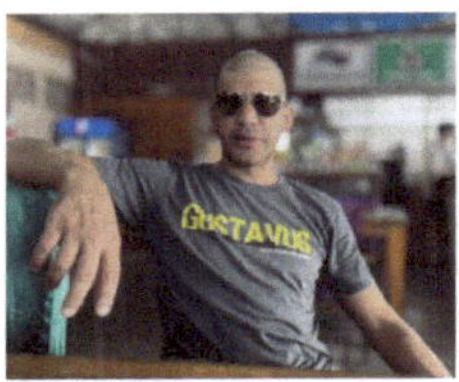

*Alessandro Asante during fieldwork in Thailand.*

**Alessandro Asante** is a bartender, chef, martial artist, and builder who co-founded the bar **MILES UP** in Thailand. More than just a venue, MILES UP was constructed from the ground up—its bar, racks, and glass shelves all hand-built by Alessandro using salvaged wooden pallets and his own tools.

His writing captures the flavor, philosophy, and fire of craft itself—blending storytelling with hands-on wisdom about smoke, spirit, and community. Raised between cultures and seasoned by travel, he pours his passion into MILES UP, where people gather beneath warm lights and wooden beams.

Asante's books *Racked & Poured: Spirits from the Shelf of MILES UP* and *The Art of Smoking: Mastering Smoke, Fire & Flavor Across Cultures* reflect his multicultural roots, culinary experience, and devotion to authenticity. His work celebrates the quiet poetry of a well-made drink, a shared meal, and the stories kindled when craft meets connection.

*The next chapter in this culinary journey, **From Fire to Flavor: Recipes Across Continents**, continues the exploration of smoke, spice, and the shared language of food around the world.*

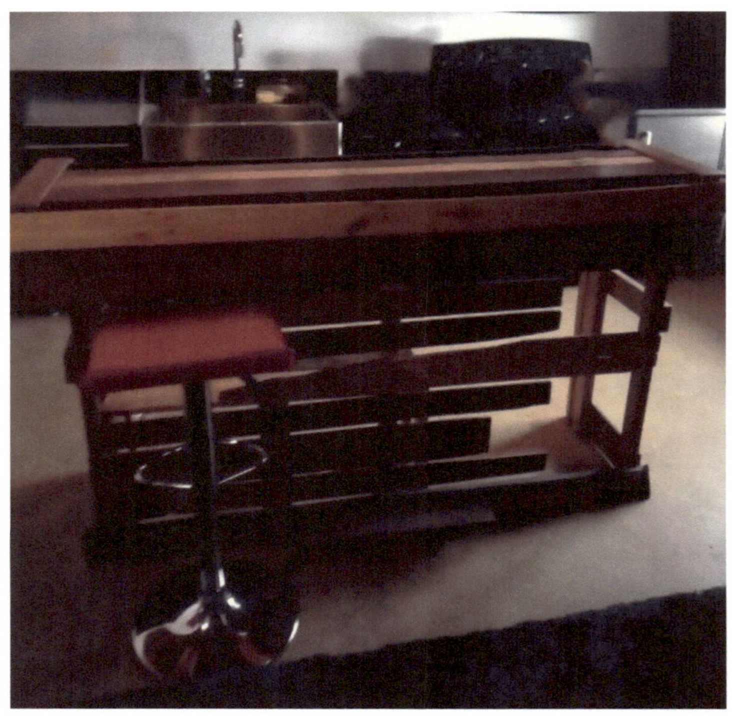

*A commissioned bar designed and built by Alessandro Asante from reclaimed wood for a DJ friend in the United States — a reflection of the craft, intention, and artistry at the heart of The Art of Smoking.*

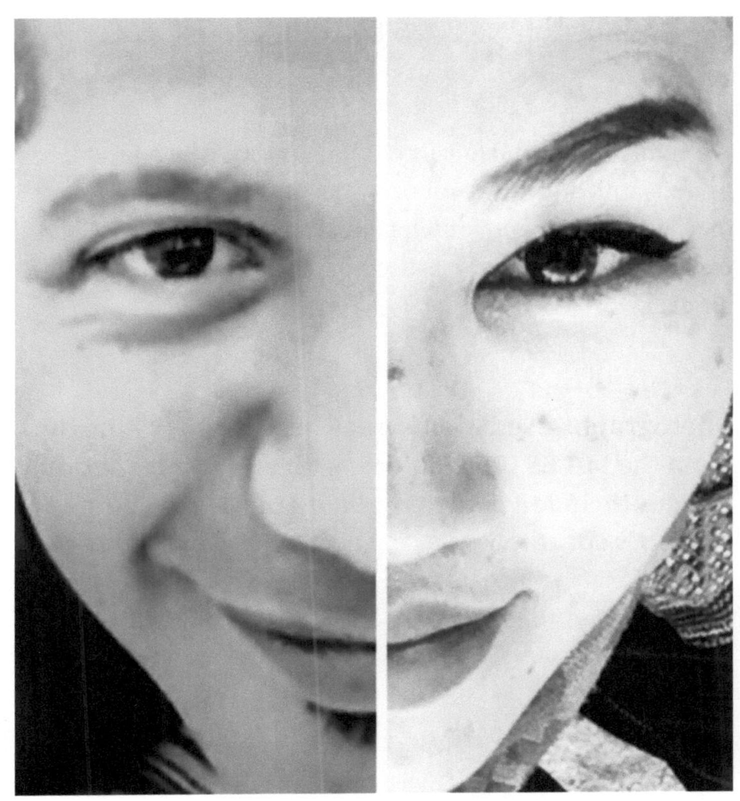

## The Two Faces of MILES UP

*The two founding faces behind MILES UP —
creators whose shared vision sparked a space
where art, craft, and culture meet.
Their collaboration shaped the spirit that
continues to guide MILES UP forward.*

**Photographs used in this book are drawn primarily from the MILES UP Archives, with select international images included courtesy of Eugenia Canaan, the project's curator.**

**Photography:** *MILES UP Archives & Eugenia Canaan*

ISBN: 978-0-9891-9329-0

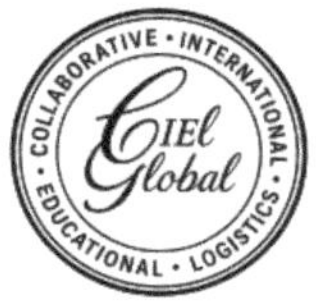

# Table of Contents

## SMOKER ANATOMY

*Every smoker speaks the*
*same language — fire below,*
*flavor above.*
*The design may change,*
*but the principle remains:*
*patience guided by heat and air.*

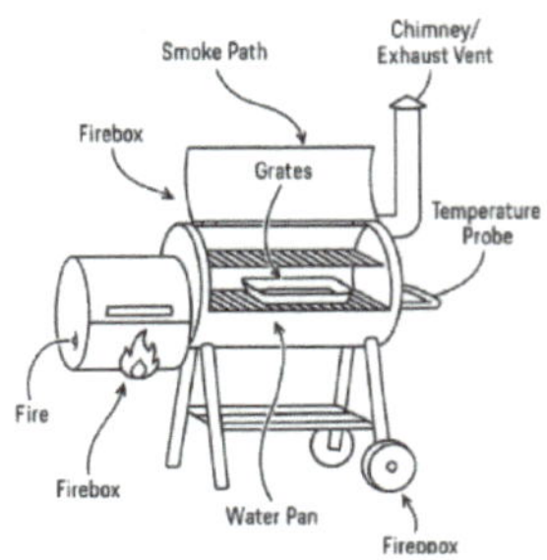


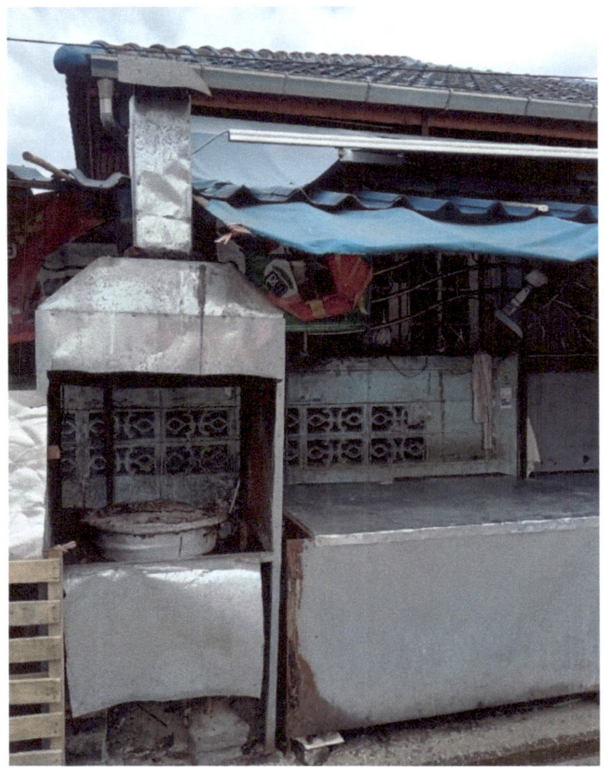

## Thai Street Ingenuity

*A humble street smoker fashioned from metal and*
*patience — proof that mastery needs curiosity more*
*than equipment.*

## DEDICATION

*In memory of Dean Raymond Gillard —*
*whose departure and this book's beginning shared the*
*same moment in time,*
*a reminder that every journey circles back to light.*

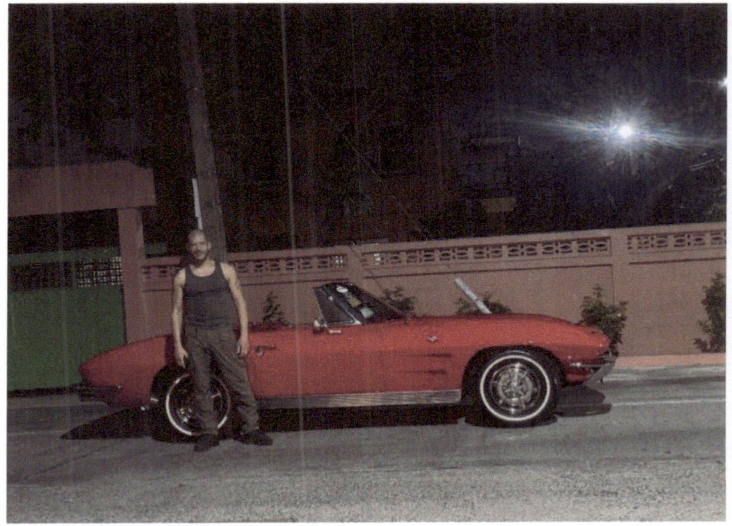

*The late Dean Raymond Gillard's car — a symbol of*
*journeys continued, with Miles at the wheel of*
*memory.*

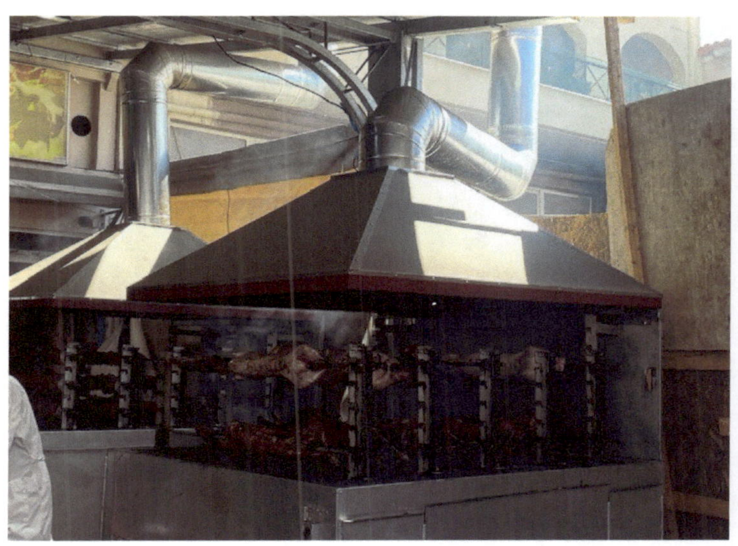

## Avlonari Smoker

*In a Greek village kitchen, modern steel meets ancient fire — a quiet bridge between reflection and design, proof that even tradition evolves through craft.*

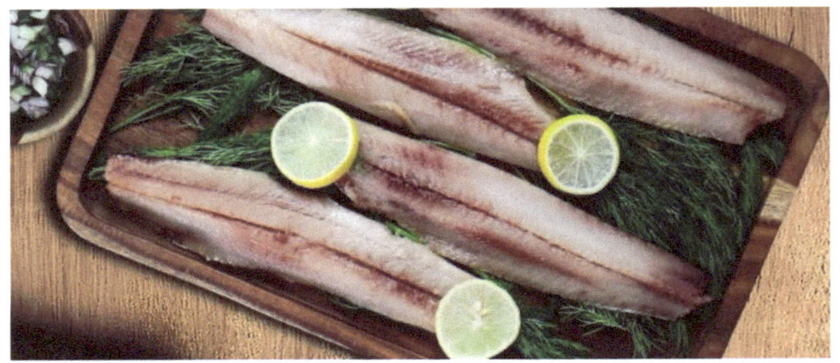

## Smoked Herring – Lebanon

*Salt, smoke, and patience — the Lebanese approach to preserving the sea's offering. Once a necessity of survival, now a delicacy of memory, served with lemon, dill, and quiet pride.*

# Chapter 1 – Smoking 101: Tools, Temps & Techniques

*"Every fire tells a story. The trick is learning its accent."* — Alessandro Asante

## The Language of Smoke

Miles Up after hours. The bar lights hum, bottles gleam, and the man behind the counter leans over a small metal box that isn't on the menu — yet. A handful of teak-wood chips sizzle; the first thin thread of smoke curls upward, dances through the glow of the bourbon shelf, and disappears into the ceiling fan.

He grins. Not bad for a first flirtation. The smoker isn't officially part of the setup — just a prototype on loan from a friend — but tonight the bar smells less like cocktails and more like possibility. The patrons have gone home; the only witnesses are a thermometer, a bourbon glass, and the faint whisper of smoke that might change everything.

## Smoking Styles: The Trinity of Temperatures

**Hot Smoking (225–275°F):** The barbecue gospel — fire that cooks and flavors at once. Brisket believers and rib romantics live here.

**Warm Smoking (90–150°F):** A slower sermon. Meat cooks gently; cheese and sausages bask instead of burn.

**Cold Smoking (under 90°F):** Where flavor whispers. Perfect for salmon, bacon, and anything you want kissed by smoke but untouched by heat.

**Hot Take:** Cold smoke is less about cooking and more about seduction.

## Essential Gear – Your Arsenal of Alchemy

Offset smokers, electric rigs, pellet grills, kamados, stovetop boxes, or a humble smoke tube — they all chase the same goal: control over chaos.
Fire is a toddler with sugar; gear is your babysitter.

**Pro Tip:** A cheap thermometer beats an expensive smoker every time. Master heat before you chase hardware.

## Fuel & Fire: The Flavor of Wood

- **Strong:** Hickory, mesquite, oak — bold, meaty, cowboy boots of the smoke world.

- **Medium:** Teak, pecan, maple — balanced, round, like jazz on Sunday.

- **Mild & Sweet:** Apple, peach, alder — fruit-kissed elegance.

Soak chips if you must, but dry wood burns cleaner and tells the truth faster.

At MILES UP, the pitmaster tosses a few local coconut husks into the mix — a Thai twist on tradition. The smoke smells faintly of palm sugar and rebellion.

## Heat Control – Zen and the Art of Vent Tweaking

Too much air and your fire rages; too little and it sulks.
Water pans add moisture, vents steer the draw, and digital probes whisper secrets your gut might miss. Think of it less as cooking and more as meditation with thermodynamics.

**Pro Tip:** Keep a notebook. Every smoke session writes its own weather report.

## Safety: Fire's Fine Print

Every pitmaster's first mistake is assuming fire behaves.
It does not — it negotiates.
Keep gear clean, fuel dry, and a spray bottle handy.
No loose sleeves, no mystery cords, and definitely no "quick nap while it smokes."
Raw meat needs cold storage, not blind faith.
Smoke adds flavor, not forgiveness.

**Hot Take:** If your smoker catches fire, congratulations — you've discovered grilling.

## Closing Reflection – The Spark Before the Flame

Tonight, the prototype smoker cools in the corner of Miles Up. He wipes his hands, sips his drink, and watches the faint trail still curling in the dim light.

He isn't serving smoked food — yet. But every great tradition starts with curiosity, and curiosity smells a lot like teak wood.

## Chapter 2 – The Smoke: Woods, Chips & Global Traditions

*"Smoke speaks every language — you just have to listen through the fire."* — Alessandro Asante

## MILES UP, Two Nights Later

The bar smells different tonight. Bottles still gleam, but the citrus bowl has been replaced with a scatter of wood chips — oak, teak, coconut husk, and a small bag labeled "sakura." A jazz playlist drifts from New Orleans to Osaka while the first wisps rise from the test rig behind the counter.

No menu, no cameras — just curiosity on slow burn. Each wood carries a memory: barbecue pits in Texas, winter docks in Norway, night markets in Bangkok. The smoke curls through them all like a passport stamp in the air.

## Wood 101 – Flavor Families

**Strong & Bold** — Hickory, mesquite, oak. The heavy hitters; they walk in wearing boots and don't apologize. Perfect for brisket, ribs, and red meat with an ego.

**Medium & Balanced** — Teak, pecan, maple. The conversationalists; smooth, a little sweet, and good with almost anything.

**Mild & Sweet** — Apple, peach, alder. Gentle persuasion; ideal for poultry, cheese, or vegetables that prefer a whisper over a shout.

**Hot Take:** If your smoke tastes like perfume, you're either burning wood that's too green — or showing off.

## The Chemistry of Smoke – Why Flavor Sticks

Wood is built from cellulose, hemicellulose, and lignin — three polite compounds that lose their manners when introduced to fire.

- **Cellulose & Hemicellulose:** Caramelize into sweet notes.

- **Lignin:** Breaks into guaiacol and syringol — the molecules that make ribs smell like heaven's campfire.

Too little oxygen and you get creosote — bitter, sticky, and unforgiving. Too much and the flavor floats away before it lands.

**Pro Tip:** Good smoke is thin and blue, not thick and white. If it looks like a fog machine, you're staging a concert, not dinner.

## Global Traditions – Where the World Smokes

### Scandinavia – Alder & Cold Air
Fish hang in wooden huts, kissed by slow alder smoke that smells of rain and fjords. The Norwegians call it patience on a hook.

### Japan – Sakura Wood & Precision
Cherry blossom wood gives a delicate, floral edge. Japanese chefs treat smoke like brushstrokes — each one intentional, never wasted.

### Middle East – Olive Wood & Memory
Lamb ribs crackle over olive logs; the aroma drifts through courtyards scented with lemon and mint. Smoke here is hospitality — it says *sit, stay, share.*

### North America – Hickory & Mesquite Pride
From Carolina pits to Texas backyards, this is competitive smoke — where temperature debates last longer than the brisket.

### Thailand – Coconut Husk Alchemy
At MILES UP, teak tables gleam under soft light as coconut husks hiss over charcoal. The scent is part sugar, part street vendor, part tropical nostalgia. It clings to the bar's wood like a promise of new dishes to come.

## DIY Blends – Mixing Woods Like Music

Smoke doesn't like monotony. Mix your woods the
way you'd mix a playlist: contrast and rhythm.

- **Apple + Hickory = "Jazz Duet"** — sweet
  meets smoky.

- **Maple + Oak = "Classic Rock"** — steady,
  crowd-pleasing, no regrets.

- **Teak + Pecan = "Slow Blues"** — mellow with
  depth.

**Pro Tip:** Keep a mason jar of mixed chips by the grill
labeled *House Blend.* Makes you sound professional,
even if you're just experimenting.


## Hot Takes & Pit Wisdom

- You can't fix bad meat with good smoke.

- Wood choice changes with weather; damp air
  loves fruit woods, dry heat needs heavier
  smoke.

- The best way to learn? Burn something once,
  taste the mistake, then write it down.

## Chapter 3 – Rubs, Brines, Cures & Marinades

*"Salt is memory; smoke is the echo."*
— Alessandro Asante


## MILES UP, The Next Afternoon

Sunlight cuts across the bar, turning bottles into stained glass. The bar's creator has traded his shaker for a mixing bowl. On the counter sit glass jars labeled *paprika, juniper, brown sugar*, and *sea salt*. A tub of water hums quietly — the first brine test.

He isn't cooking for guests today; he's experimenting for the future. The air smells like curiosity seasoned with ambition.


## Dry Rubs – Alchemy in Powder Form

Salt, sugar, and spice: three ingredients that decide whether meat sings or sulks.
A good rub wakes up the surface, drawing moisture outward before it melts back in.

### Classic Ratio

- 2 parts salt

- 2 parts sugar (brown for depth, white for bark)

- 1 part spice blend (paprika, pepper, garlic, cumin, chili)

Massage it like an apology — firm but sincere.

**Pro Tip:** Keep one "signature" spice constant across dishes; it becomes your flavor fingerprint.
**Hot Take:** If your rub needs twenty ingredients, you're hiding from commitment.


## Wet Brines – Water That Remembers

Brining is patience in liquid form. It keeps proteins tender and flavors honest.

**Base Formula:**
1 gallon water | 1 cup salt | ½ cup sugar + aromatics (bay, citrus peel, juniper).
Substitute part of the water with cider, beer, or wine for personality.

Soak poultry overnight, pork for a day, and seafood just long enough to feel admired, not drowned.

**Pro Tip:** Cool your brine before the dunk. Rushing the preparation can spoil what could have been great if you had waited just a bit longer.

**Pro Tip (Pu's Kitchen Wisdom):** As Pu likes to warn new patrons, unless you're conditioned for Thai heat, don't order "Hot." Even her "Mild" has ambition.

## Cures – When Smoke Meets Science

Cold-smoked foods need insurance. That's where curing salt (sodium nitrite) steps in — preserving color, flavor, and safety.

**Basic Cure:** Salt, sugar, pink salt #1 (¼ tsp per pound).
Massage onto bacon, ham, or fish; let rest 5–7 days in the fridge, flipping daily like a slow conversation.

Rinse, dry, and smoke low. The result: flavor that hums like jazz in a cellar bar.

**Hot Take:** Patience is the real ingredient. Rushing a cure is culinary counterfeit.


## Marinades – Liquid Personality

Where brines preserve, marinades flirt. Acid or enzyme breaks down texture while oil and herbs whisper complexity.

**Base Types**

- **Bright & Tangy:** Citrus, vinegar, garlic, chili — for seafood and lighter meats.

- **Deep & Herbal:** Oil, soy, rosemary, mustard — for beef, lamb, or duck.

Don't drown your food; coat it lightly and give it time to think.

**Pro Tip:** Reserve a small portion before the meat goes in — it makes a built-in finishing sauce.

**Global Notes – How the World Seasons**

- **Japan:** Miso & mirin marinades — umami as religion.

- **Caribbean:** Allspice, lime, and Scotch bonnet fire — joy and danger intertwined.

- **Middle East:** Yogurt, cumin, lemon — tenderness through tang.

- **Scandinavia:** Salt & dill cures — clarity through cold.

- **Thailand:** Palm sugar and fish sauce alchemy — sweet, funky, balanced chaos.

MILES UP smells faintly of every continent now, and the pitmaster grins like a traveler who never left his bar.


**Closing Reflection – The Season of Patience**

Curing, brining, marinating — all are acts of waiting. Smoke may be the headline, but salt writes the story.

He wipes down the counter, labeling each jar with a grin. Tomorrow, the smoker returns. The experiments will leave the bar and meet the flame.

## Chapter 4 – Smoking Beef:
## Brisket, Ribs, Roast & Jerky

*"Beef doesn't rush — it negotiates with the flame."*
— Alessandro Asante

### MILES UP, Late Afternoon

The smoker hums like a slow heartbeat behind the bar. A quiet bourbon sits nearby while patrons gather like disciples around the first slab of brisket MILES UP has ever seen.

The meat goes in, the lid drops, and the conversation shifts from small talk to reverence. Firewood stacks like a library behind the counter — oak, teak, and a few Thai coconut husks for luck. The bar's transformation has begun: from spirits to smoke.

### The Gospel of Beef Smoke

Beef loves patience. Its fibers are stubborn, its fat deliberate. You can't charm it with heat; you have to persuade it.

Every cut has its own opinion about time: brisket wants half a day, ribs want attention, and chuck roast just wants to be noticed.

Collagen melts at 160°F, flavor deepens around 200°F, and somewhere between science and surrender, you find magic.

**Pro Tip:** The best smokers check their watches less than their wood.


## Texas Brisket – The Pilgrimage

Every pitmaster's rite of passage starts with a brisket and a long weekend.
Rub it simple: half salt, half black pepper. That's it.

Set the smoker to 225°F. Twelve to sixteen hours later, wrap it in butcher paper when it "stalls" — that purgatory around 160°F where evaporation cools it down just to test your faith.
When it hits 203°F, pull it, rest it for an hour, and try not to weep.

At MILES UP, the pitmaster slices his first test brisket paper-thin. The smoke ring glows pink like dawn on steel.

**Hot Take:** Brisket isn't cooked when it's done; it's cooked when it forgives you.


## Beef Ribs – Smoke and Swagger

If brisket is poetry, beef ribs are sculpture — each bone a cathedral beam.
Dust with your favorite rub, smoke low and slow for six to eight hours, oak wood whispering encouragement.

When the bark crust forms, you're in the sweet spot
— texture that cracks, flavor that lingers.

**Pro Tip:** Don't rush the rest. Steam ruins bark faster
than applause ruins humility.

## Smoked Chuck Roast – The Blue-Collar Brisket

Same personality, half the price.
A chuck roast is beef's everyday hero — humble,
marbled, and forgiving.

Rub it generously, smoke it six to seven hours until it
reaches 200°F, and slice against the grain.

**Hot Take:** Chuck roast is what brisket wishes it
could be on a tight schedule.

## Pastrami – Old World Meets Smokehouse

Start with corned beef — soak it to calm the salt, rub
it with cracked pepper and coriander, and smoke at
225°F until it reaches 203°F inside.

The scent is equal parts Lower East Side and MILES
UP — deli nostalgia with a tropical wink.

**Pro Tip:** Steam pastrami after smoking for extra
tenderness — tradition with a side of innovation.

## Beef Jerky – Smoke You Can Pocket

Thin slices, lean cuts, long patience. Marinate 24
hours, smoke at 165°F for five hours.
The goal isn't chewiness; it's character.

**Pro Tip:** Don't over-marinate. Jerky that tastes like soy sauce is just sodium in denial.

## Global Sparks – Where the Flame Travels

- **Argentina:** *Asado* masters swear by patience and posture — the grill is a religion, and smoke its gospel.

- **Korea:** *Bulgogi* meets smoke through sweetness and fire, proving that marinades and heat can coexist peacefully.

- **Middle East:** Smoked kebabs brushed with pomegranate molasses — ancient barbecue diplomacy.

Miles Up nods to them all. A whisper of spice here, a wood blend there. Smoke without borders, flavor without ego.

## Pro Tips & Pit Wisdom

- Trim fat, but never pride.

- Keep notes — smoke logs are the travel diaries of flavor.

- Cold meat catches smoke better than warm.

- Every smoker has moods; learn them before you lecture them.

**Hot Take:** The moment you think you've mastered beef, start over — it changes every season.

**Closing Reflection – The Patience of Iron & Flame**

When the smoker lid finally lifts, the bar fills with a low, primal perfume.
Slices are carved, passed to eager patrons, and for a heartbeat, nobody speaks.

Beef has found its altar, fire its disciple, and Miles Up its next identity.
Smoke, salt, and time — the holy trinity realized.

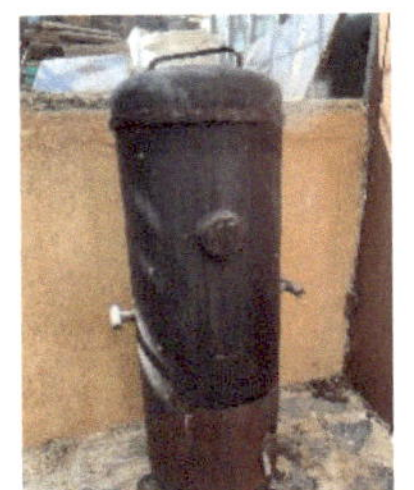

**Greek Ingenuity**

*An old metal smoker repurposed for new fires —*

*humble yet precise, a testament to resourceful hands and patient heat. Inset: marinated pork slowly taking on its smoky character — Greek tradition alive in scent and skill.*

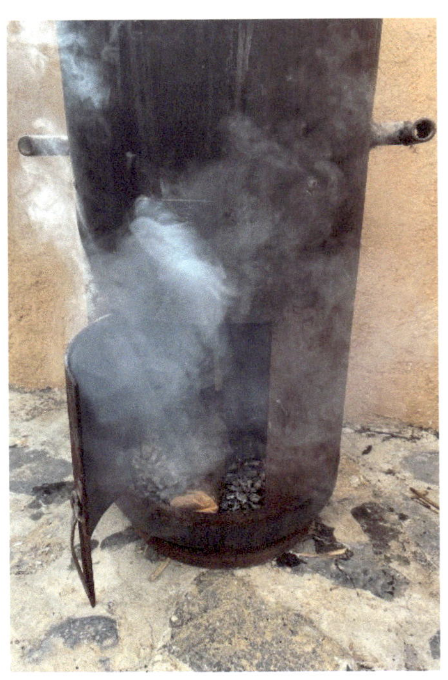

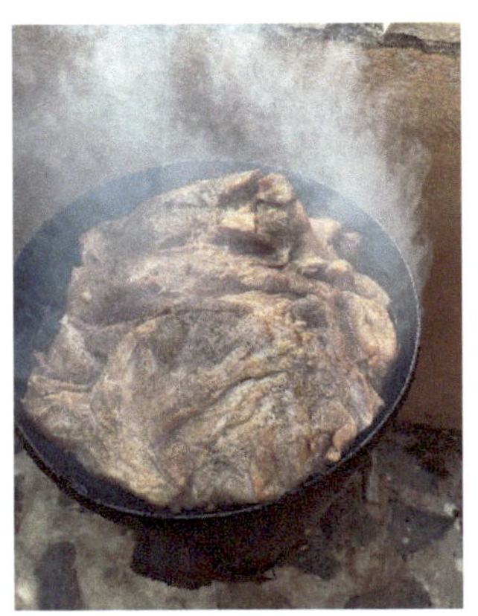

*Reward of slow fire –*

*proof that time*

*still has taste*

20

## Chapter 5 – Smoking Pork: Shoulder, Belly, Ham & Sausage

*"Where there's smoke and sweetness, there's usually a pig nearby."* — Alessandro Asante

## MILES UP, Night Before Service

The smoker has moved from curiosity to centerpiece. Tonight, it hums out back, its glow bouncing off the bottles inside. The pitmaster leans on the counter, notebook open, jotting times like gospel: shoulder, belly, ham.

The air outside carries apple wood and quiet confidence. Inside, the patrons debate sauces. The bar feels less like a watering hole now and more like a workshop of patience and appetite.

## Smoked Pulled Pork – The Crowd-Pleaser

Shoulder, butt, or picnic cut — it doesn't matter; they all forgive.
Rub with paprika, brown sugar, salt, garlic, mustard powder.
Smoke low at 225°F until 165°F, wrap tight, and cruise to 203°F.

Let it rest an hour before you pull; every fiber will surrender on cue.

**Pro Tip:** Spritz every couple of hours with apple juice or cider vinegar — hydration is happiness.

**Hot Take:** Pulled pork is less a recipe, more a trust exercise between you and time.

## Pork Belly Burnt Ends – Candy for Carnivores

Cube it, rub it, smoke it three hours uncovered.
Then drown in glaze, wrap in foil, and return for two more hours of sticky redemption.

When the experiment ran behind MILES UP, even the grocer from next door wandered in "just to check the smell."

**Pro Tip:** Honey in the glaze gives you lacquer; molasses gives you mystery.

## Smoked Ham – Old World Resurrection

Already-cooked ham? Glaze and reheat to 140°F.
Raw ham? Brine 7–10 days, rinse, then slow-smoke like a hymn.

Pineapple glaze is fine, but a maple-mustard crust with clove spikes turns nostalgia into art.

**Hot Take:** Ham is Christmas waiting for an excuse.

## Smoked Bacon – The Seven-Day Patience Plan

Cure pork belly 7 days with salt, sugar, and pink salt #1.
Rinse, dry overnight, and smoke at 175°F until it hits 150°F internal.
Slice thin, fry crisp, resist the urge to brag.

**Pro Tip:** Save the rendered fat; it's liquid seasoning for everything else you cook this year.

## Smoked Sausage – Links of Legacy

Chorizo, kielbasa, andouille, bratwurst — smoke turns them from humble to heroic.
Hot or cold, natural casings preferred, patience mandatory.

**Pro Tip:** Hang sausages so they don't touch — airflow equals even color and flavor.
**Hot Take:** If your sausage bursts, don't curse — call it "artisan rustic."

## Global Notes – Smoke Travels on a Passport of Pork

- **Spain:** Chorizo kissed by oak; paprika doing the talking.

- **Germany:** Applewood-smoked brats under beer foam.

- **China:** Cantonese lap cheong cured in rice wine — sweet smoke poetry.

- **Thailand:** Sai ua from Chiang Mai — lemongrass, chili, and pride in a coil.

- **American South:** Hickory halos around pulled pork sandwiches big enough to change your faith.

At MILES UP, a note in the margin reads *"Smoked Sai Ua Slider?"* — and the pitmaster grins.

## Pro Tips & Pit Wisdom

- Don't peek too often — heat leaves faster than the return of confidence.

- Sugar burns; use fruit woods for sweetness instead.

- Rest every cut before you serve.

- Never argue with a pitmaster holding tongs.

## Closing Reflection – The Alchemy of Sweet Smoke

By midnight, the pork shoulder has fallen apart under its own weight.
He tears a strand with his fingers, dips it into his vinegar sauce, and nods slowly.

Pu's traditional Thai dishes already anchor the bar's menu; when the smoked selections join them, patrons will taste a new balance of fire and flavor.

The bar lights glow soft and amber, and for a moment Miles Up smells like home for every traveler who has ever followed the scent of smoke.

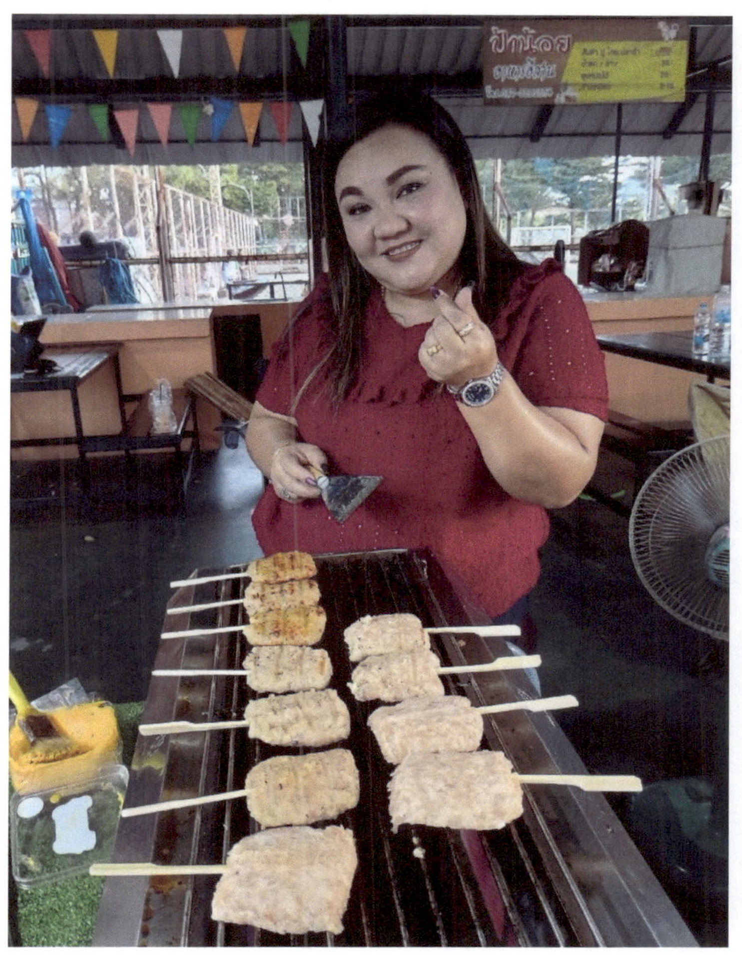

## Street Skewers

*Behind every smoky aroma stands a smile — a vendor turning sizzling pork skewers with practiced ease, embodying the heart and hospitality of Thai street food.*

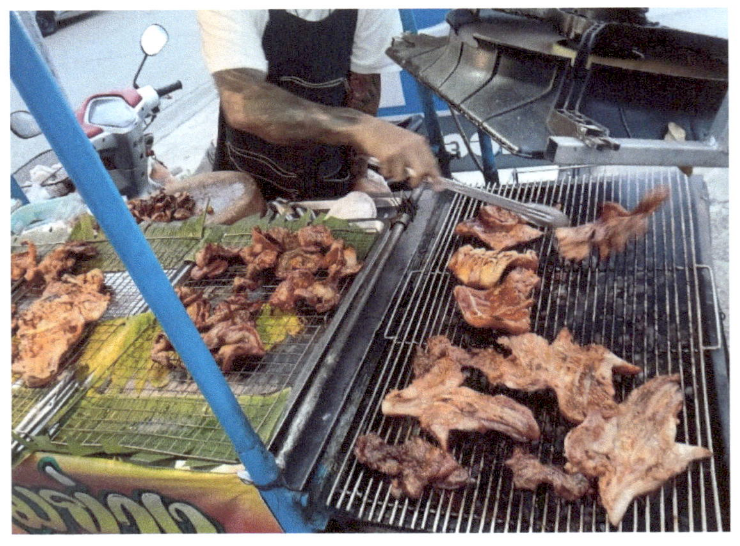

## Master of the Grill

*Flame, tongs, and timing — every turn on the grill a dialogue between fire and flavor.*

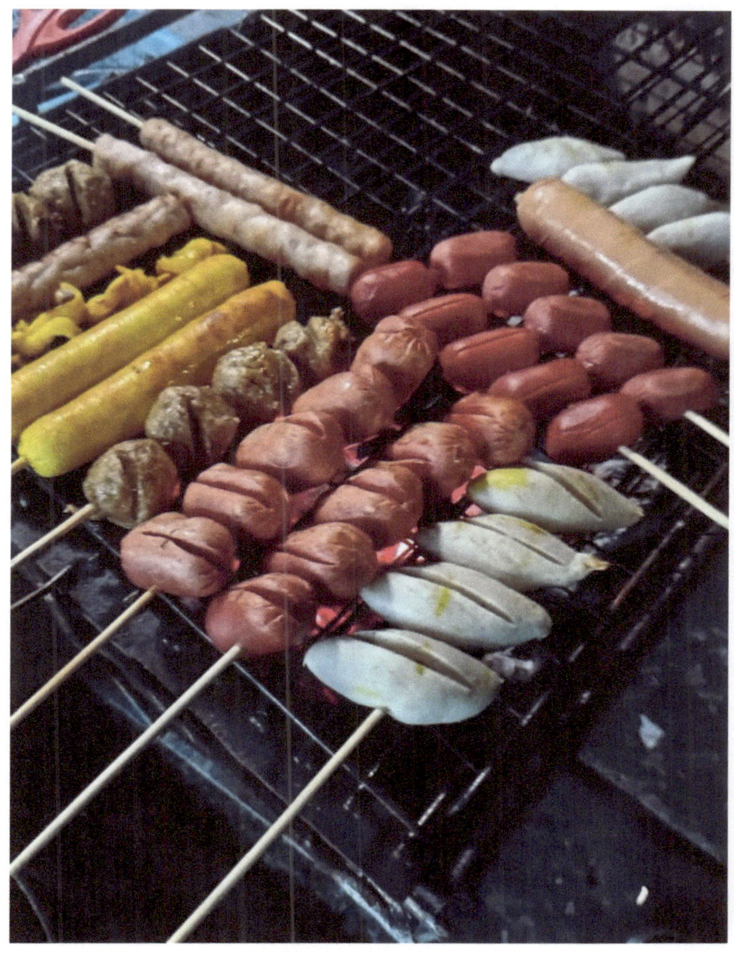

**Mixed Skewers on the Grill**
*Street skewers sizzle over open coals – spice, smoke, and color mingling in Thailand's evening air.*

## Mushrooms – Earth Under Smoke

Big caps like portobellos act as flavor sponges.
Brush with soy sauce and butter; smoke 45 minutes
at 230°F.

**Pro Tip:** Dice leftovers into risotto — instant depth.
**Hot Take:** Mushrooms don't need meat to feel
important.

## Corn – Sunlight in a Husk

Soak ears 30 minutes in water, husks on. Smoke 1
hour at 250°F. Peel back, butter, return for 10
minutes of glory.

**Pro Tip:** Sprinkle chili-lime salt for a Thai street-
food echo.
**Hot Take:** Butter is diplomacy between smoke and
sweetness.

## Eggplant – Silk and Shadow

Slice thick, salt lightly, rest 15 minutes to draw
bitterness. Pat dry, oil, and smoke at 240°F for 45
minutes.

**Pro Tip:** Blend smoked eggplant with tahini —
instant baba ghanoush that whispers campfire.
**Hot Take:** Eggplant smoked right could convince a
carnivore to reconsider.

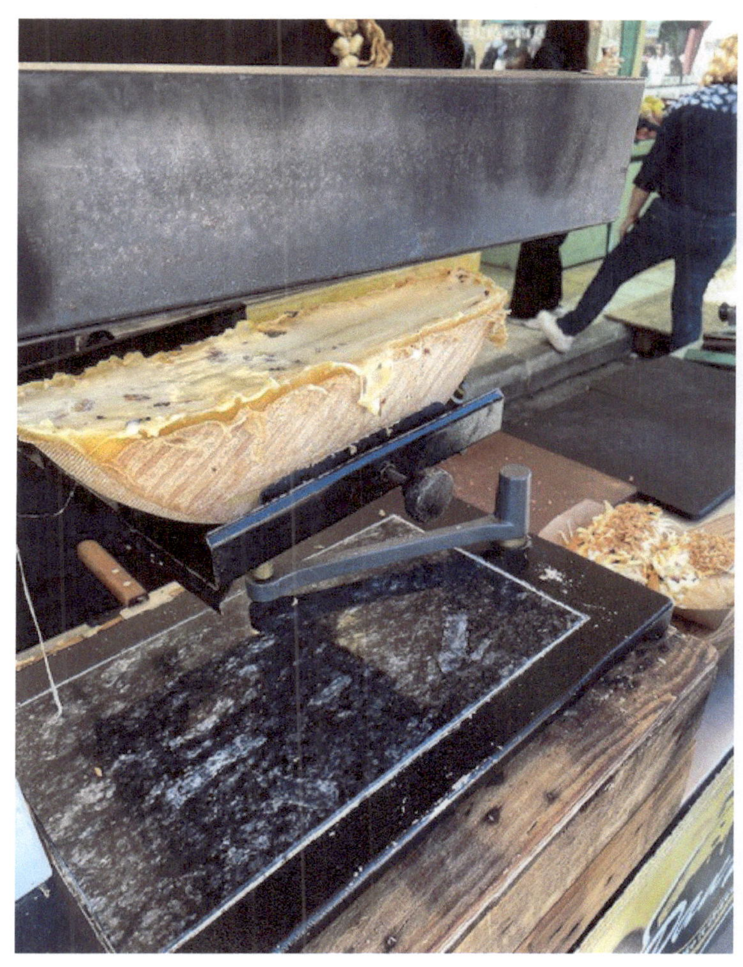

## Raclette in Motion – Greece

*Cheese softens under the flame, its surface caramelizing as each scrape reveals the next layer of melt.*

## Cheese – Patience and Precision

Cheese loves cold smoke, not heat.
Keep temps under 90°F; any hotter and you're
hosting fondue.

Use a smoke tube with ice tray inside the chamber.
Cheddar, gouda, and mozzarella work best. Smoke 2
hours, rest in the fridge 24 hours before slicing —
the flavor deepens overnight.

**Pro Tip:** Wrap in parchment, not plastic; smoke
needs to breathe.

**Hot Take:** Fresh-smoked cheese is proof that time
forgives everything.

## Global Notes – Smoke Without Borders

- **Italy:** Mozzarella di bufala under olive wood
  — soft cloud, salted sunlight.

- **India:** Smoked paneer with garam masala —
  aroma meets geometry.

- **Mexico:** Corn and cotija with lime and chili
  — street food meets heaven.

- **Thailand:** Smoked tofu with lemongrass and
  tamarind glaze — sweet meets savory in
  equilibrium.

Inside MILES UP, the bar now glows like a painter's palette. Pu peeks from the kitchen, grinning — even she approves of smoke without fire.

## Closing Reflection – The Soft Side of Smoke

Not everything that meets the flame must surrender. Some ingredients only need a whisper.

The pitmaster wipes the counter, arranging bright, smoked slices on a board. For a moment, the bar feels like a garden that learned to breathe teak.

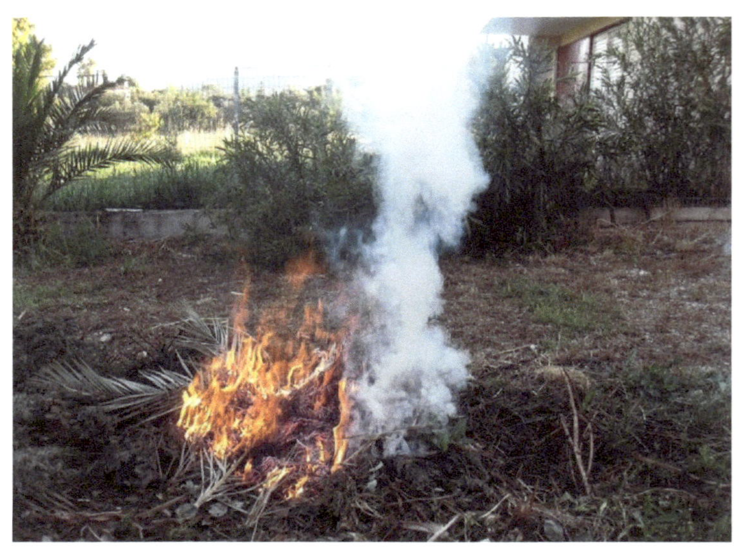

## Open Fire – Greece

*An open flame in the family olive orchard —*
*heat and instinct working together in one of*
*cooking's oldest forms.*

## Chapter 6 – Smoking Poultry: Chicken, Duck & Turkey

*"A little fire makes a bird sing louder."*
— Alessandro Asante

### MILES UP, After Dark

By now, smoke wasn't just a technique—it was a language, and MILES UP was learning to speak it. Fans hum behind the bar, the flimsy wooden doors half-slid shut but never really closing. The first wave of teachers from the international school set aside their bags, order cold beer, and talk about their day while the pitmaster checks the vents on the smoker. Outside, night gathers thick as teak smoke and chili.

### Chicken – The Gateway Bird

Brine, rub, and smoke at 225°F until the skin snaps. Butter halfway through; applause guaranteed.

**Pro Tip:** Fruit wood or light teak keeps flavor honest.

**Hot Take:** Suspense belongs in movies, not undercooked chicken.

## Duck – Smoke Meets Silk

Pierce, render, and smoke at 225°F until 165°F.
Palm-sugar glaze for a Thai wink.
**Pro Tip:** Save the fat—gold for potatoes.
**Hot Take:** Duck doesn't share rack space politely.


## Turkey – The Patience Test

Brine overnight with citrus and lemongrass. Smoke
250°F, 30 min per lb.
**Pro Tip:** Butter under skin, always.
**Hot Take:** Turkey rewards calm hands.


## Global Notes

**South**: Buttermilk chicken; China: Tea-smoked duck;
**Middle East**: Sumac quail; Thailand: Coconut-
smoked chicken.


By 10 p.m. the bar fills—music, laughter, plates
passed hand to hand.


## Closing Reflection – The Quiet Hours

Poultry teaches patience. Smoke curls through the
open gaps as the pitmaster wipes the counter,
already thinking of fish waiting in ice.

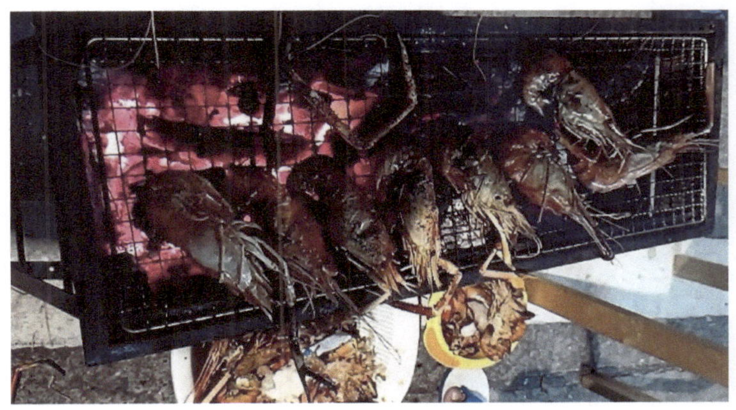

## Thai Prawns on the Grill

*Night heat and glowing coals – a ritual of flavor*
*where fire, smoke, and sea meet in perfect simplicity.*

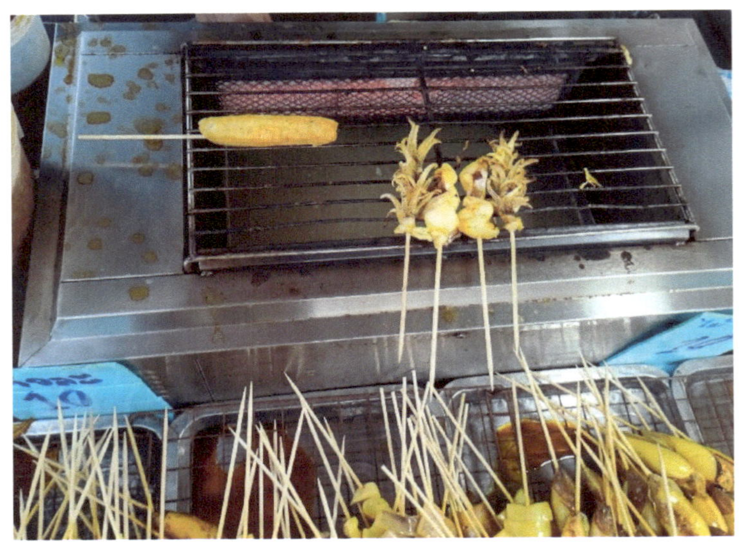

## Grilled Squid

*Fresh from the sea to the skewer — grilled squid sizzling over open flame, brushed with chili sauce and served by the street, a Thai favorite from coast to city.*

## Chapter 7 – Smoking Fish & Shellfish: Salmon, Trout, Shrimp & Mussels

*"Where there's water, there's always something worth smoking."* — Alessandro Asante

### MILES UP, Near Midnight

The second wave of regulars claim their stools. A visiting DJ fades Thai pop into Chicago blues; smoke mingles with rhythm. On the back table: salmon fillets, shrimp, mussels—the sea arriving after dark. Patrons drift in, drawn to smoke, spirits, and stories.

### Salmon – The Classic

Brine 1 hour (¼ cup salt + ¼ cup brown sugar). Smoke 225°F, 1 hour per inch. Brush with honey late.
**Pro Tip:** Sweet glaze seals moisture.
**Hot Take:** Good salmon whispers.

### Trout – The Stream's Secret

Stuff with lemon and dill.
Smoke 200°F for 45–60 min.
**Pro Tip:** Seek translucence, not grill marks.
**Hot Take:** Trout forgives speed, not distraction.

### Shrimp – Smoke in Seconds

Brine 15 min, smoke 200°F for 20 min.

**Pro Tip:** Skewer sideways.

**Hot Take:** Be ready before it is.

### Mussels – Shells That Speak

Pan with wine + butter, foil-cover, smoke 225°F 30 min.

**Pro Tip:** Lemongrass = Thai accent.

**Hot Take:** Closed shells stay closed.

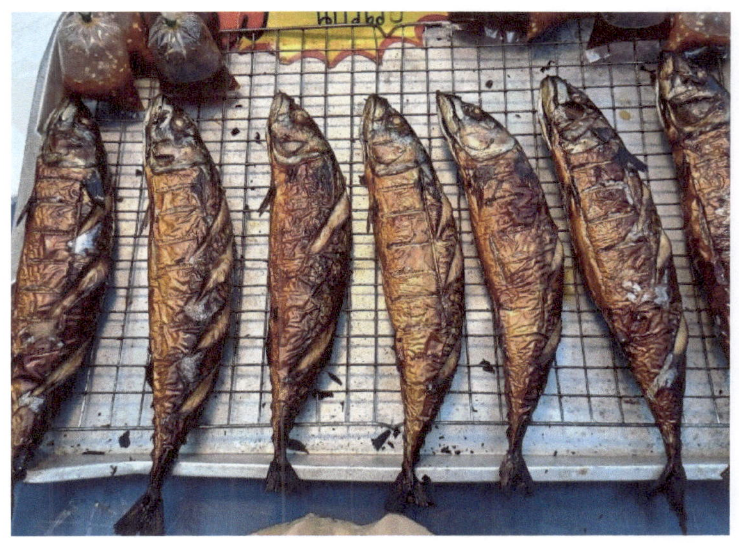

## Grilled Mackerel Display

*Char-grilled mackerel laid out in neat rows — a humble yet beloved staple found in Thai markets, best enjoyed with spicy dipping sauce and warm sticky rice.*

**Global Notes**

Nordic cold-smoked salmon; Japan's cedar-smoked eel; Mediterranean olive-wood mussels; Thailand's coconut-lime shrimp.
Music rises; people dance between tables, guitars answering the DJ's beat.

**Closing Reflection – The Taste of Tides**

Seafood humbles haste. The pitmaster lifts the lid, a breath of brine and teak escaping to the street. Inside, the bar sways like a boat at anchor.

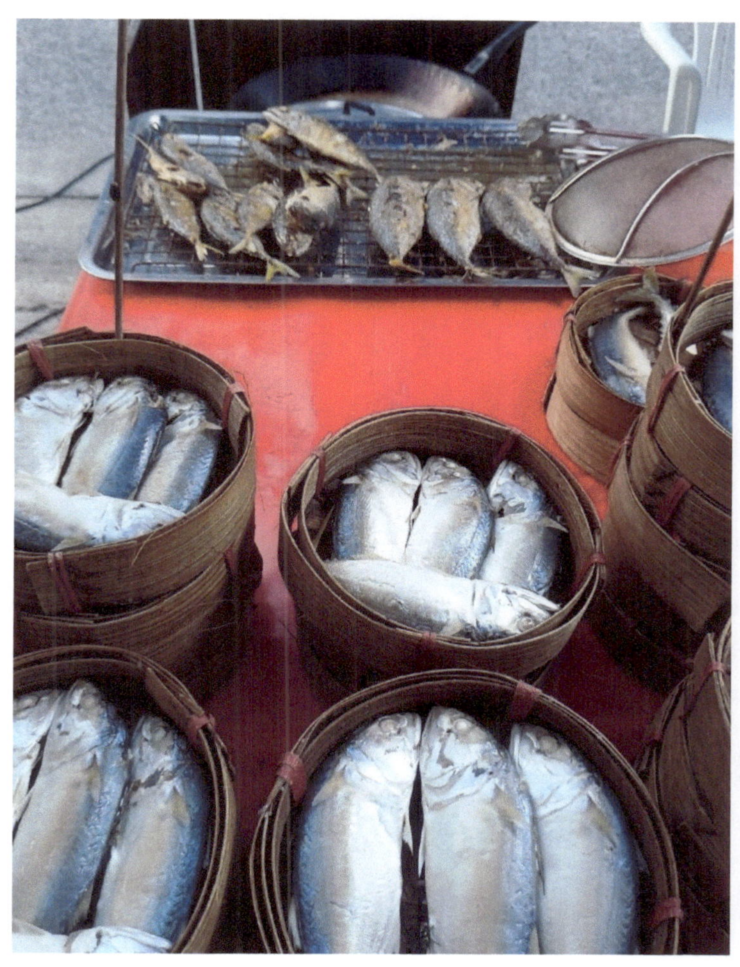

## Steamed and Fried Mackerel Baskets

*Steamed mackerel nestled in bamboo baskets, ready for market or grill — a timeless Thai staple known for its freshness, simplicity, and unmistakable aroma.*

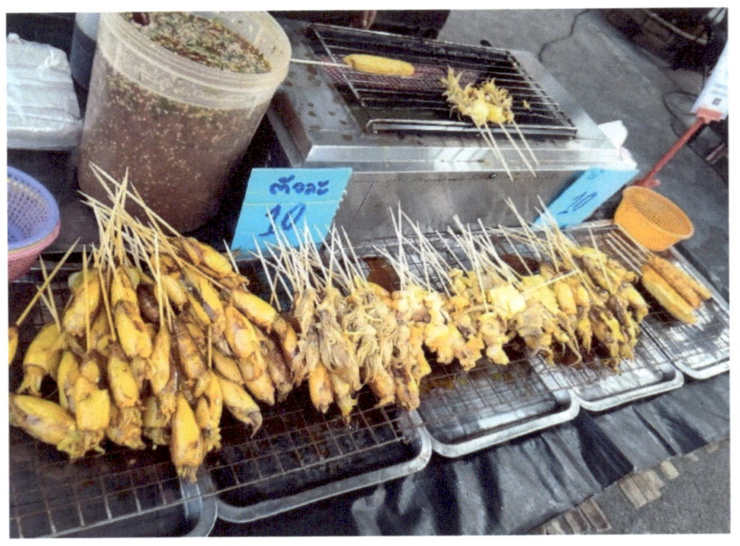

## Street Stall at Midmorning

*Rows of squid ready for the grill, each skewer waiting its turn beneath the vendor's watchful flame.*

## Chapter 8 – Smoking Game & Exotic Meats

*"Wild flavor teaches us what patience tastes like."*
— Alessandro Asante


### MILES UP, After Midnight

The music has eased from dance to groove. Regulars trade places with late-night wanderers; a few teachers drift back for one last beer. The smoker's glow paints the alley behind the bar, where the pitmaster tests new cuts — venison, boar, quail. The air hums with teak and jazz guitar.


### Venison – Lean & Legendary

Marinate overnight in olive oil, red wine, juniper.
Smoke 225°F to 135°F internal.
**Pro Tip:** Wrap mid-way; foil is forgiveness.
**Hot Take:** Venison rewards attention, punishes ego.


### Wild Boar – Smoke with Attitude

Rub paprika, brown sugar, mustard powder. Smoke 250°F 4–5 hours to 190°F internal.
**Pro Tip:** Mop with apple juice + soy sauce.
**Hot Take:** Boar doesn't compromise.

## Quail – The Gentle Rebel

Brine 2 hours with lime, pat dry, rub lemongrass.
Smoke 200°F 45 min.
**Pro Tip:** Use a basket; quail falls apart when happy.
**Hot Take:** One per person is manners.


## Lamb – Ancient Smoke, Eternal Faith

Rub olive oil, garlic, rosemary; rest overnight. Smoke
250°F 4 hours; finish with pomegranate molasses.
**Pro Tip:** Fruit woods keep it bright.
**Hot Take:** Every bite is a sermon.


## Global Notes

**Africa** – Antelope with tamarind;
**Australia** – Kangaroo under eucalyptus;
**Europe** – Hare with mustard glaze;
**Thailand** – Boar ribs over teak and husk.


Out front, laughter swells again. Someone starts a
rhythm on an empty bottle; Miles answers with a
few guitar chords.

**Closing Reflection – The Wild Within**
Game carries the earth in its veins. Smoke just
reminds it who it is.


The pitmaster leans back, satisfied; the night still has
hours left to tell its stories.

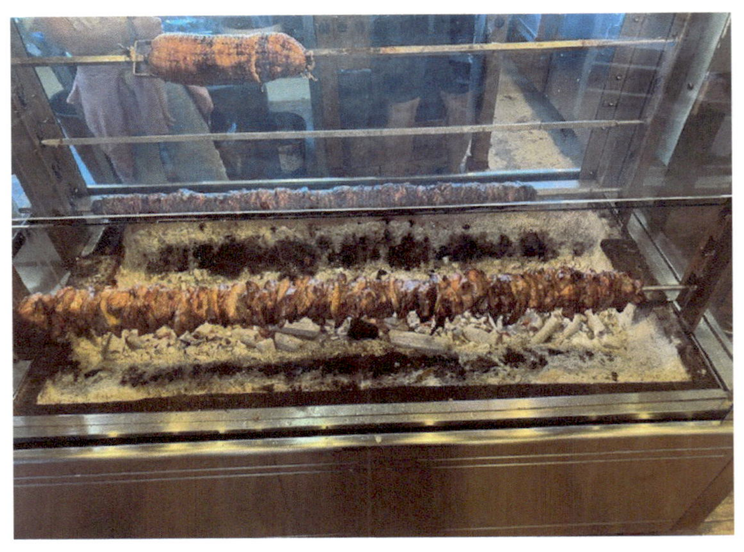

**In Greece, smoke meets heritage on the spit —**
*from the layered indulgence of kontosouvli to the rustic ritual of kokoretsi.*
*Each rotation provides the deep satisfaction of marinated food kissed by flame.*

## Chapter 9 – Smoking Vegetables & Cheese

*"Even the quietest ingredients have something to say under smoke."* — Alessandro Asante

### MILES UP, Toward Dawn

Fans stir slow air through open planks. A few night-owls linger over late plates. Pu hums behind the counter, tasting sauces, while the pitmaster lines trays of color — peppers, corn, mushrooms, eggplant, and a wheel of brie. The music softens to blues. Everyone here feels at home.

### Vegetables – The Unexpected Canvas

Brush lightly with oil + salt. Smoke 225–250°F, 30–60 min.
**Pro Tip:** Finish on hot grill for color.
**Hot Take:** Ashy veg means lazy fire.

### Mushrooms – Earth Under Smoke

Brush soy + butter; smoke 45 min at 230°F.
**Pro Tip:** Dice into risotto tomorrow.
**Hot Take:** They don't need meat to matter.

## Corn – Sunlight in a Husk

Soak 30 min, smoke 1 hr at 250°F, butter, return 10 min.
**Pro Tip:** Chili-lime salt for a Thai echo.
**Hot Take:** Butter is diplomacy.

## Eggplant – Silk and Shadow

Salt 15 min, pat dry, smoke 240°F 45 min.
**Pro Tip:** Blend into smoked baba ghanoush.
**Hot Take:** Could convert a carnivore.

## Cheese – Patience and Precision

Keep under 90°F for 2 hrs; rest 24 hrs in fridge.
**Pro Tip:** Parchment, not plastic.
**Hot Take:** Time forgives everything.

## Global Notes

Italy – Olive-wood mozzarella; India – Smoked paneer; Mexico – Corn & cotija; Thailand – Smoked tofu with tamarind.
Pu steps out laughing, handing a plate to a late guest. "Try this," she says, "not too hot… maybe."

## Closing Reflection – The Soft Side of Smoke

Not everything meeting fire must surrender. Some only need a whisper.
The pitmaster arranges the bright slices, and for a moment the bar feels like a garden that never closed.

## Chapter 10 – Global Smoked Dishes: Japan, Scandinavia, Middle East & More

*"Every culture has its own way of talking to fire."*
— Alessandro Asante

### MILES UP, Pre-Dawn

The last wave drifts in from other bars — musicians, cooks, travelers who know this place never truly closes. Music fades to guitar and soft percussion; bottles clink; smoke lingers like a final verse.

### Japan – Precision in the Mist

Sakura-wood smoke around salmon with mirin.
**Pro Tip:** Light smoke, thin slices.
**Hot Take:** Restraint is a spice.

### Scandinavia – Patience on Ice

Cold-smoked fish below 80°F.
**Pro Tip:** Preservation is poetry.
**Hot Take:** Snow tastes like time.

### Middle East – Smoke as Hospitality

Olive-wood under lamb and eggplant, pomegranate molasses drizzle.
**Pro Tip:** Let acid follow smoke.
**Hot Take:** A shared grill is older than language.

## Mediterranean – Sunlight Meets Salt

Fish and fennel over vine trimmings.
**Pro Tip:** Olive oil keeps it bright.
**Hot Take:** Simplicity is courage.

## Thailand – Fire with a Smile

Coconut husk + lemongrass; Pu's chilies whisper
warnings.
**Pro Tip:** Balance spice and sweet.
**Hot Take:** Mild is myth.

## Mexico – Street Smoke & Soul

Mesquite ribs with lime.
**Pro Tip:** Add citrus after smoking.
**Hot Take:** Smoke is celebration.

## Global Notes

Across continents, smoke means patience,
transformation, joy.
The pitmaster closes his notebook; around him,
friends finish their drinks slowly.

## Closing Reflection – The World in One Bar

Every culture wrote its own verse of the same poem:
wood + heat + hope.
Miles Up breathes softly, its fans spinning the night's
last song. *Home doesn't really close.*

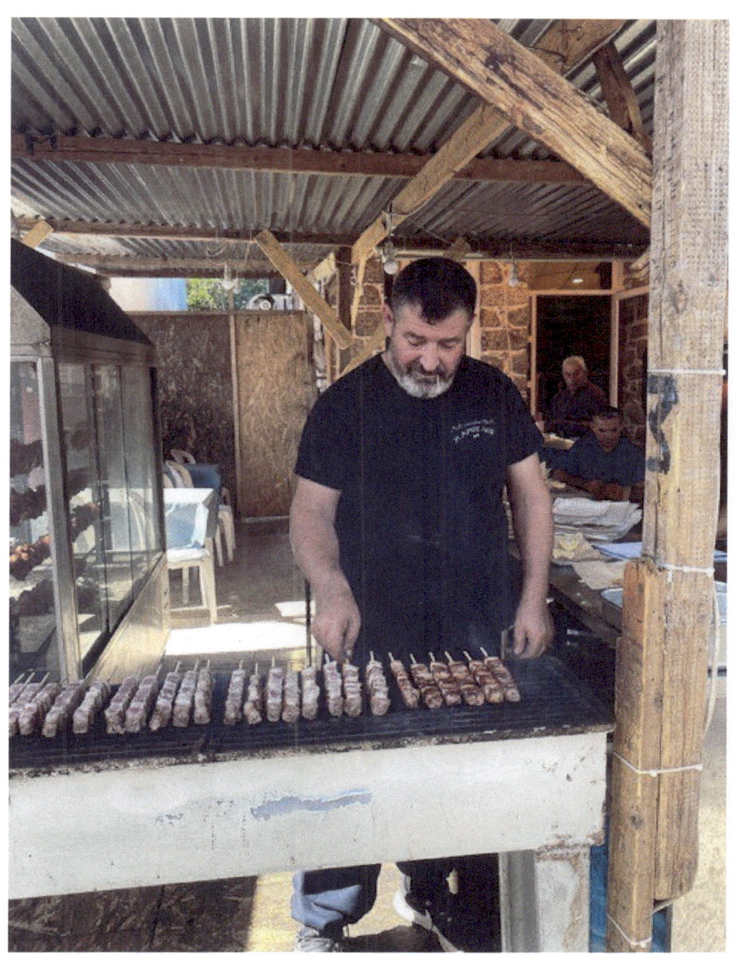

**Avlonari Souvlaki**

*From Bangkok to Avlonari, the rhythm of smoke is the same — patient, fragrant, elemental. Here, on the island of Evia, the grillmaster's focus mirrors that of his Thai counterparts: fire as language, flavor as memory.*

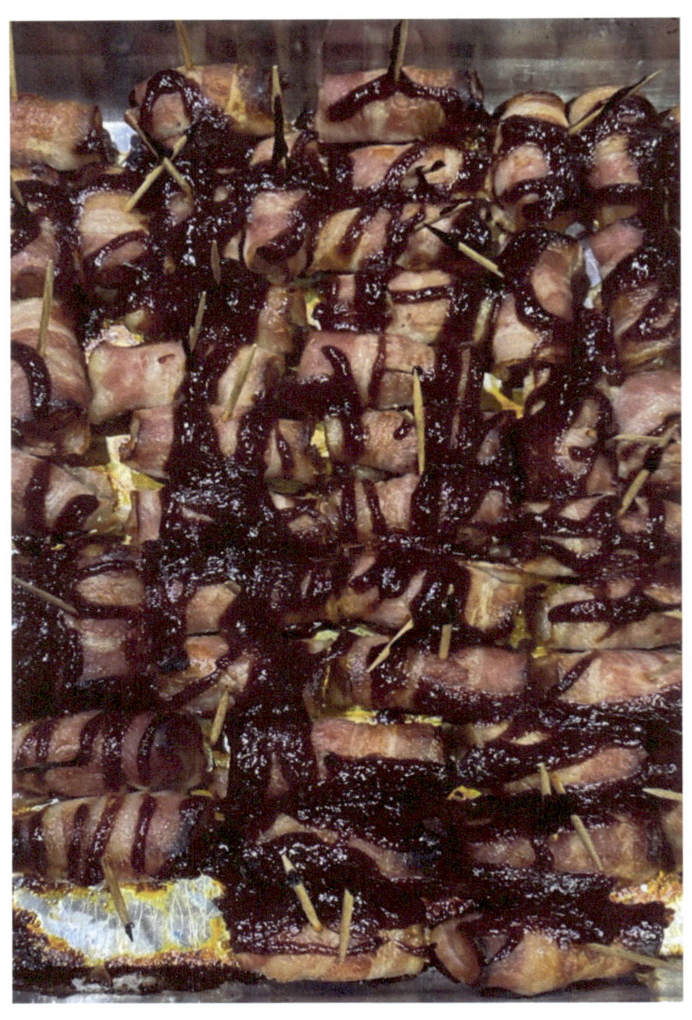

## Bacon-Wrapped Bites

*Born from a Greek evening and an American craving — sweet glaze over smoky bacon, turning backyard celebration into crowd-pleasing comfort.*

## Chapter 11 – DIY Smoking Projects: Cold Smoke, Homemade Bacon & Charcuterie

*"Mastery starts the day you stop buying smoke and start making it."* — Alessandro Asante

Cold Smoke – The Whisper Technique
Cold smoke isn't cooking; it's perfume. Temperature: below 90°F (32 °C).

**You'll need:**
- A separate firebox or smoke tube
- Flexible ducting or a length of metal pipe
- A cooler, cabinet, or sealed box for the food
- Thermometer and patience

**How-to:**

1. Light a small bed of chips in the firebox; let it settle into a smolder.
2. Feed the smoke through the ducting into your chamber.
3. Vent lightly — think exhale, not cough.

Try it first with cheese, nuts, or salt. Each absorbs aroma fast and forgives early mistakes.
**Pro Tip:** A bowl of ice inside the chamber keeps temp low and humidity friendly.
**Hot Take:** If you see flames, you're confessing to grilling.

## Homemade Bacon – Seven Days to Redemption

Base Cure (per 5 lb/2.3 kg belly):
¼ cup kosher salt
¼ cup brown sugar
1 tsp pink salt #1
**Optional:** black pepper, bay leaf, maple syrup drizzle

**Steps:**

1. Rub cure evenly; seal in bag or pan.
2. Refrigerate 7 days, turning daily.
3. Rinse, pat dry, rest overnight uncovered for a pellicle.
4. Hot-smoke at 175°F (80 °C) to 150°F internal.
5. Chill and slice thin.

**Pro Tip:** Save rendered fat — it's liquid memory.
**Hot Take:** Store-bought bacon is just an apology waiting to happen.

## Charcuterie – The Long Game

Where bacon is a week, charcuterie is a season.

**Starter Kit:** pork shoulder or belly, salt, sugar, curing salts #2, spices, and time.

**Basic Roadmap:**

1. Cure the meat with salt + spice blend 10–14 days.
2. Rinse, hang in a cool (55°F / 13 °C), humid (70%) place for weeks or months.
3. Weigh weekly — 30% weight loss = safe and ready.

**Pro Tip:** Label every batch; memory is not a preservation method.
**Hot Take:** Mold is not the enemy — ignorance is.

## Final Reflection – From Spectator to Maker

You've learned to taste smoke; now you create it. Every hiss of wood, every cured slice, is a handshake between craft and courage.

Keep notes. Keep faith. And never forget — the best flavor is the one you earned.

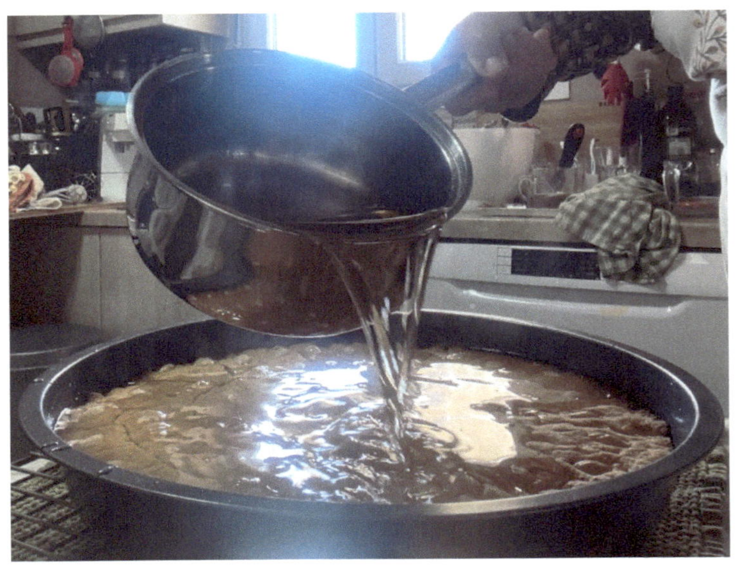

## When Syrup meets Heat

*When the mountain wind said no to smoke, the kitchen said yes to sweetness.*
*Basboosa (Nammoura) rising — proof that transformation wears many flavors.*

# Chapter 12 – Pro Tips, Tools & Troubleshooting

*"Fire doesn't forgive, but it does teach — if you're paying attention."* — Alessandro Asante

## Gear That Earns Its Keep

A great pitmaster doesn't need a showroom — just reliable tools and respect for them.

### Essentials:
- Thermometers
- Tongs & Gloves
- Vents & Dampers
- Spray Bottle
- Logbook

**Pro Tip:** Write it down before the bourbon.
**Hot Take:** A clean grill grate is sexier than a shiny smoker.

## When Smoke Misbehaves

**Problem:** Bitter flavor, dark soot on food.
**Cause:** Incomplete combustion or green wood.
**Fix:** Open the vents; use seasoned wood.

**Problem**: Fire won't stay lit.
**Cause:** Too little oxygen or damp fuel.
**Fix:** Crack the door, feed smaller splits.


**Problem:** Meat's dry but still tough.
**Cause**: Heat too high early on.
**Fix:** Low and slow.


**Pro Tip:** The stall at 160°F isn't failure; it's science.
**Hot Take**: Patience costs less than ruined meat.


**The Flavor Equation**
Salt + Smoke + Time + Rest.
**Pro Tip**: Let your meat rest wrapped at least 30 minutes.
**Hot Take:** If you slice early, you're spilling flavor onto the cutting board.


**Closing Reflection** – The Fire Listens
You'll know you've matured when you stop fighting the flame and start conversing with it.
It doesn't speak fast — but it never lies.

## Chapter 13 – Sauce & Side Pairings

*"Smoke is the story; sauce is the signature."*
— Alessandro Asante

## The Philosophy of Sauce
Sauce doesn't rescue — it reveals.
**Pro Tip:** Always taste before saucing.
**Hot Take:** If it swims, it sins.

## Classic Companions
**Sweet Heat Glaze** – brown sugar, chili, cider vinegar, butter.

**Maple-Mustard Harmony** – maple syrup, Dijon, apple juice, thyme.

**Tangy Carolina Dip** – vinegar, crushed pepper, honey.

**Thai Fusion Finish** – fish sauce, lime, palm sugar, chili flakes.

**Pro Tip:** Label every jar with date and batch.
**Hot Take:** A blender is a philosopher's stone.

**Sides that Hold Their Ground**

**Smoked Corn Salad** – lime, cilantro, chili.

**Grilled Pineapple & Mint** – beside pork or duck.

**Charred Eggplant Spread** – puree with tahini.

**Roasted Sweet Potatoes** – maple glaze.

**Pro Tip**: Don't overfill your table.
**Hot Take:** Color on the plate isn't decoration — it's appetite psychology.

**Pairing by Element, Not Habit**

**Sweet smoke**: add acid.

**Spicy smoke**: add cool.

**Earthy smoke**: add fresh.

**Bright smoke**: add depth.

**Closing Reflection** – The Table After the Fire
Good sauce invites conversation, good sides hold it together.
When the dishes are cleared and the embers fade, what remains is the sharing.

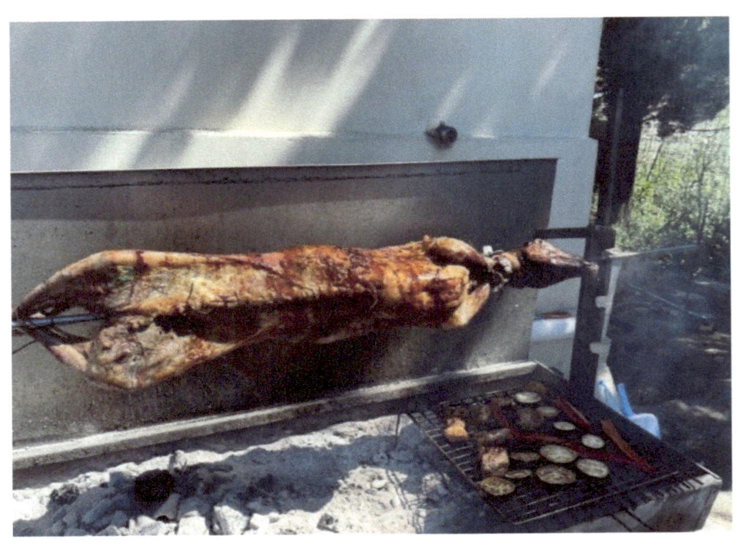

## Easter Sunday in Greece

*The lamb turns slowly over white coals, a ritual of renewal where fire, family, and faith share the same breath of smoke.*

## Chapter 14 – Sauces of Smoke – A Global Palette

Before we close, I wanted to share the sauces that have followed me from one fire to the next — recipes written not on paper, but in memory and heat.
Each carries a region's rhythm, a cook's instinct, and the same quiet conversation between smoke, sweetness, and time.

### Texas Bold

Tomato-based and fearless — smoky, pepper-forward, and lightly sweetened.
Start with **twice as much tomato as vinegar**, and stir in brown sugar until it balances the tang. Add onions, garlic, black pepper, and a touch of cayenne for courage.
**Simmer** slowly until the sauce thickens and darkens. **Cool and rest overnight** — smoke meets patience here. Keeps well for a week refrigerated.

### Louisiana Rhythm

Brown sugar hums against bourbon and a whisper of brandy. Add Creole spice, Worcestershire, and a splash of vinegar to keep it dancing. Sweet, smoky, and slightly rebellious — a sauce that turns every bite into a second line.
**Simmer** 15–20 minutes, just until the alcohol fades and the sugars caramelize. **Store covered** up to 10 days; flavor deepens daily.

**Tennessee Balance**

Where sweet meets tart. Start with **equal parts ketchup and cider vinegar**, add brown sugar, and your secret weapon — **a splash of Coca-Cola or orange juice**. A spoonful of mustard keeps the peace.

**Brush thick on ribs** and let it glaze to gold. **Warm before using**; it thickens as it cools.


**Carolina Gold**

Born from mustard and heritage — bright, tangy, alive.

Blend **yellow mustard with honey, brown sugar, and cider vinegar** until smooth and glossy. Add chili flakes or paprika for a deeper hue.

**Simmer lightly** for 5–10 minutes, just enough to marry the flavors. **Serve warm or chilled.**


**Missouri Sweet Smoke**

Between Kansas City and St. Louis lies balance: tomato, vinegar, brown sugar, molasses, and lemon.

**Simmer low and slow** until it clings to the spoon like memory. The longer it rests, the thicker the story.

**Refrigerate up to two weeks**; brush liberally on ribs, brisket, or anything worthy of a second kiss from the flame.


**Final Note from the Pit**

*I've shared these foundations so you can make them your own. Don't follow too closely — experiment, adjust, and taste. Burn a few, fix a few, and before long you'll find your own voice in the smoke. Happy smoking.*

## Chapter 15 – The Last Ember

*"Every flame fades, but the lesson lingers."*
*— Alessandro Asante*

The smoker is cold now. Tools hang clean, the counter wiped, the notebook closed. The air still carries a trace of oak and citrus — faint, honest, earned.

This isn't a goodbye from the fire, only an intermission. Smoke, after all, is a traveler; it moves from wood to meat to memory. You've learned to build it, guide it, and trust it.

The author of *Racked & Poured* and *The Art of Smoking* will soon turn his attention to flavor without flame — recipes gathered from the markets, coasts, and kitchens that shaped the journey.

So close the vents. Pour one last drink.
And when tomorrow's smoke drifts upward, take a moment to listen — the ember still speaks your name.

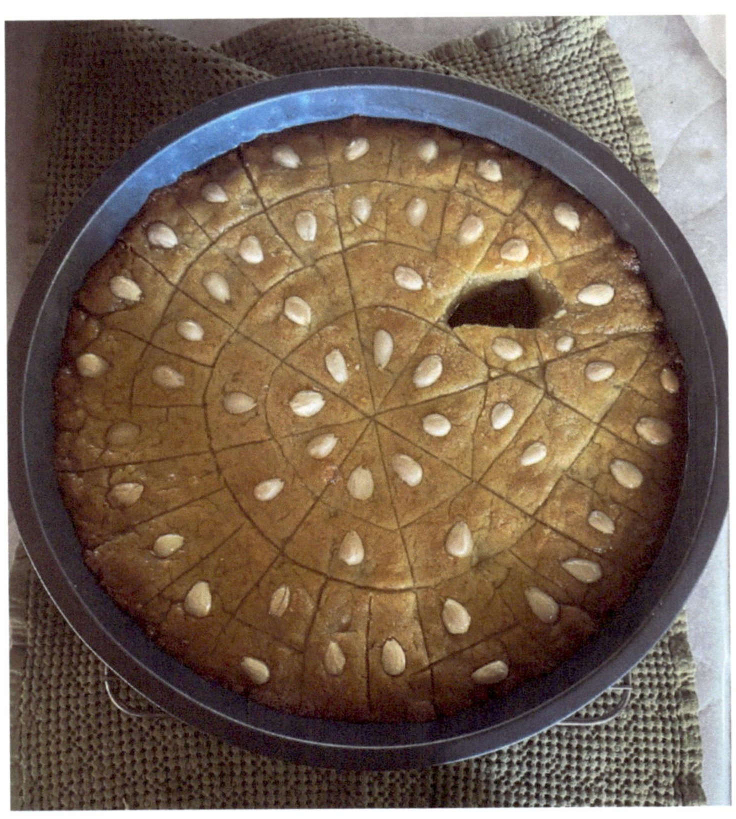

## Couldn't Resist a Bite

*Just to be sure the syrup settled right.*
*Sweetness shared — a quiet encore after the smoke.*

**Cultural Note**: *Basboosa (also known as Nammoura) is a fine semolina dessert common across the Middle East and North Africa, including Egypt, Lebanon, and Greece. This version adds orange blossom, fig syrup, and a hint of Tsipouro — the curator's own twist on tradition.*

# FIRE ACROSS BORDERS

*Across continents and kitchens, the language of smoke is universal. Whether rising from a street stall in Bangkok, a terrace grill in Lebanon, or a holiday hearth in Greece, fire becomes both tool and teacher — uniting craft, culture, and community.*

*Each flame tells a story of adaptation: local woods, inherited recipes, shared tables. Together they remind us that food, like fire, travels — carrying memory and meaning wherever it lands.*

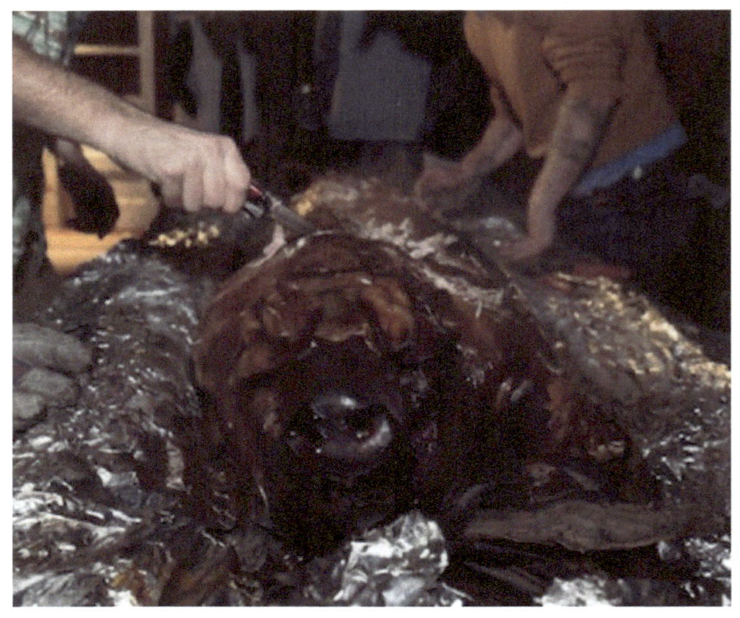

## Cajun Cochon de Lait – Louisiana, USA

*Smoke, foil, and flame — the hallmarks of a Louisiana gathering. The cochon de lait is more than a roast; it's a ritual of music, patience, and storytelling, where community rises with the scent of hickory and oak.*

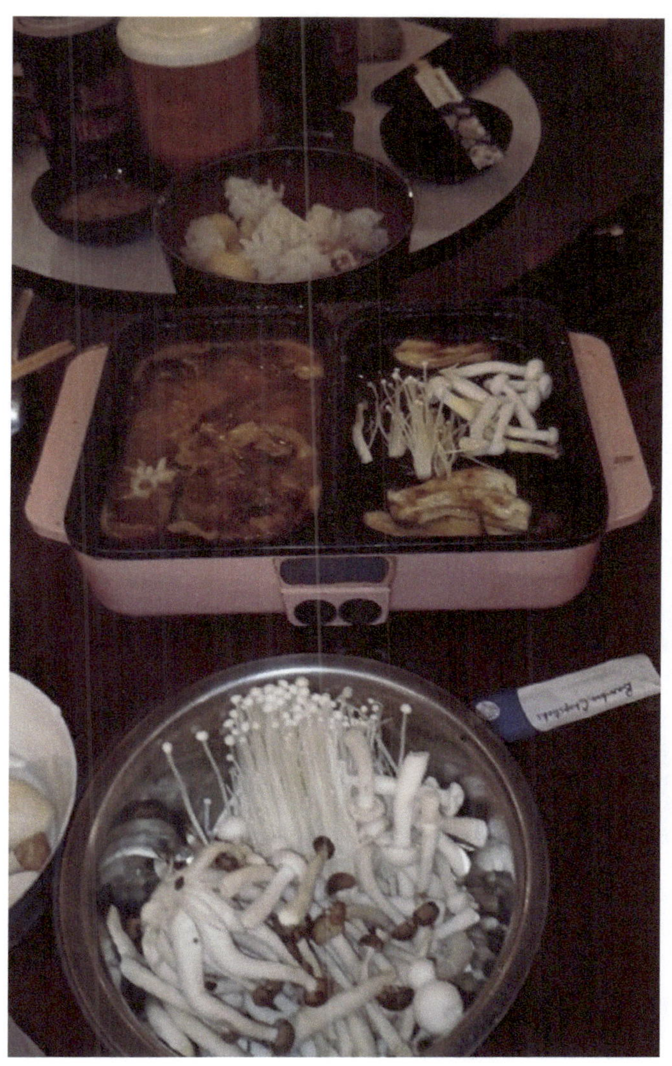

## MILES UP Buffet – Bangkok Region

*Where the bar becomes a kitchen and smoke meets conversation. At MILES UP, buffets blend experiment with comfort — a fusion of flavors from east and west, simmered in the rhythm of community and curiosity.*

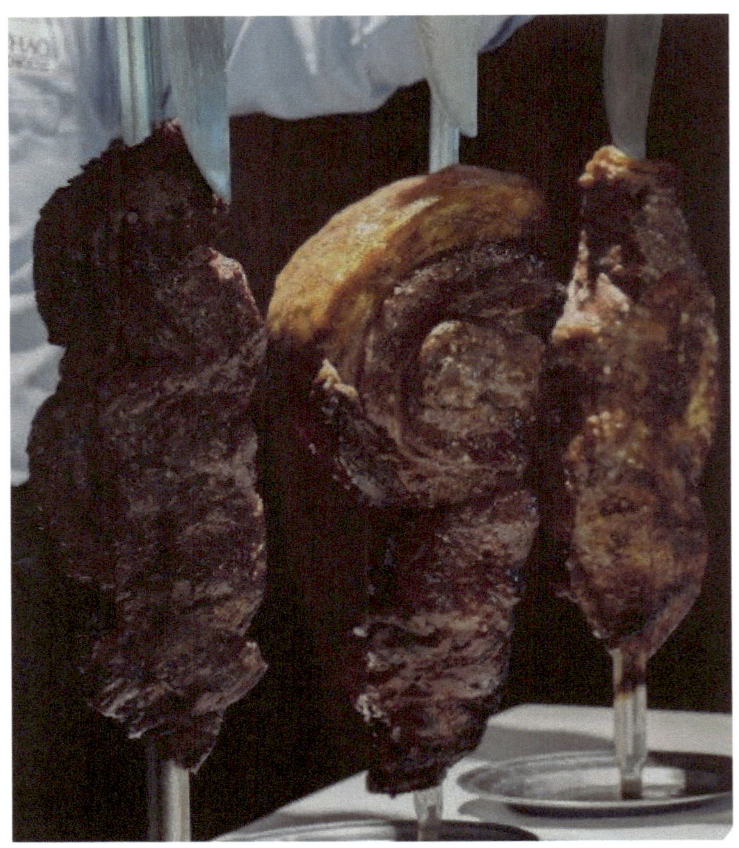

## Fogo de Chão – Brazil

*At Brazil's famed Fogo de Chão, the fire never sleeps.*
*Skewers of picanha turn slowly over coals, each slice*
*a balance of heat, patience, and pride. For those who*
*love smoke, this is ritual — a feast shaped by flame.*

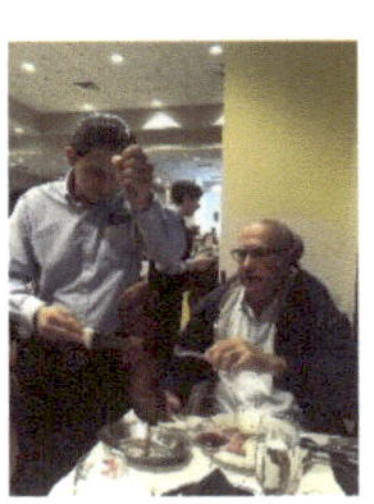

*A family celebration at*
*Fogo de Chão, Minnesota —*
*a taste of Brazil shared abroad.*

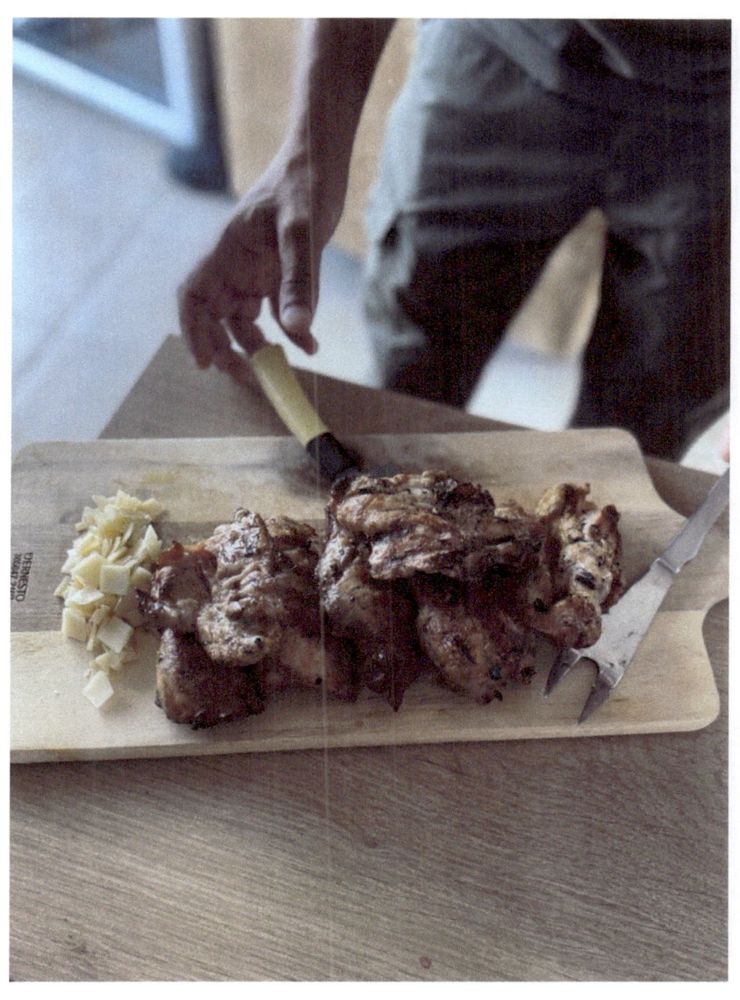

**Charbroiled Chicken, Greece**

*Grilled and shared in silence — a meal offered not for celebration, but for comfort. Smoke rose softly that day, carrying both memory and mercy.*

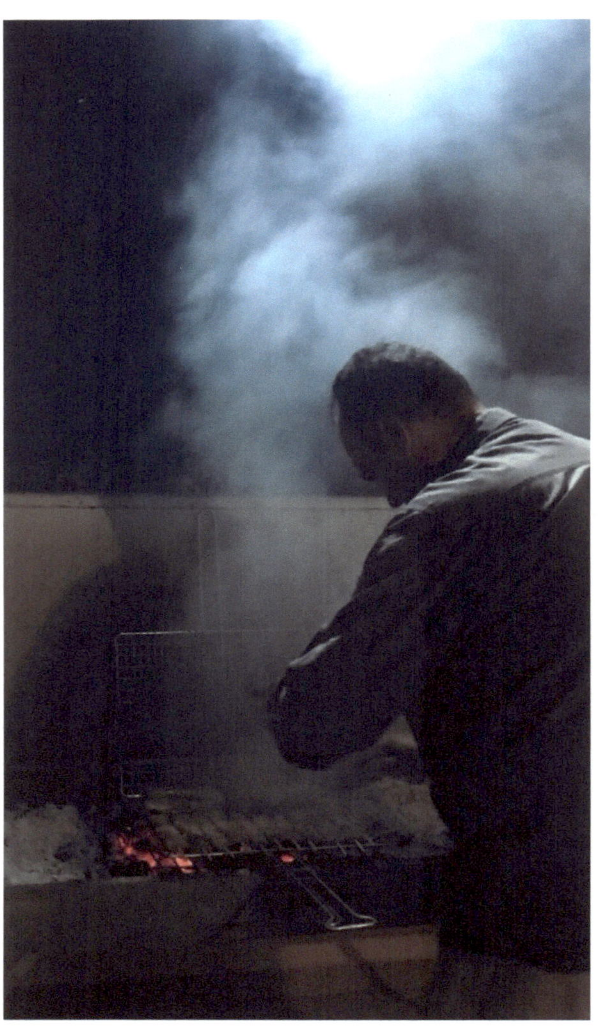

## Smoked Souvlaki – Greece

*Charcoal, marinated meat, and the steady hand of a village grill master — the essence of Greek street smoke. Simple ingredients, patient heat, and a hint of lemon transform the ordinary into the unforgettable.*

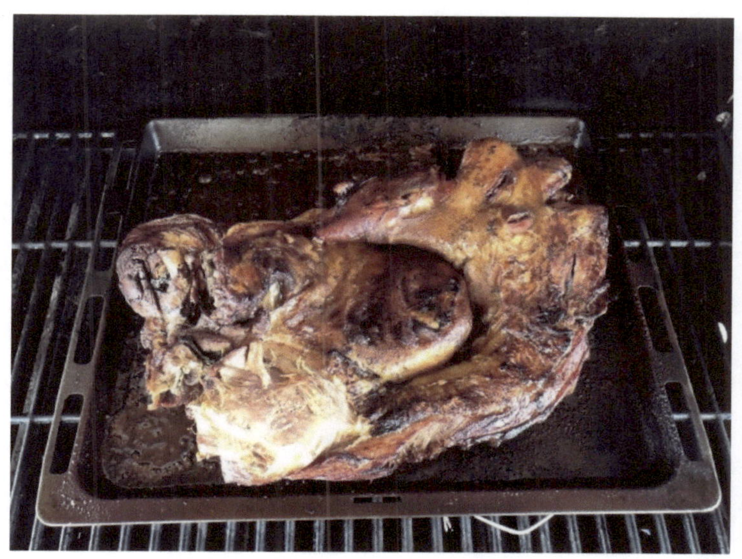

## Christmas Bouti Gourounopoulo – Greece

*On a winter morning in Greece, the pork leg — "bouti gourounopoulo" — roasts slowly over embers, its crackling skin sealing in centuries of family tradition. The aroma mingles with laughter and the distant calanda — festive carols sung door to door — as families gather around the fire to share warmth, food, and faith.*

***Cultural Note***: *The calanda (καλάντα) are traditional Greek carols sung by children and families during Christmas, New Year, and Epiphany. Carrying small metal triangles or drums, singers move from house to house, offering blessings of prosperity and joy in exchange for sweets or coins.*

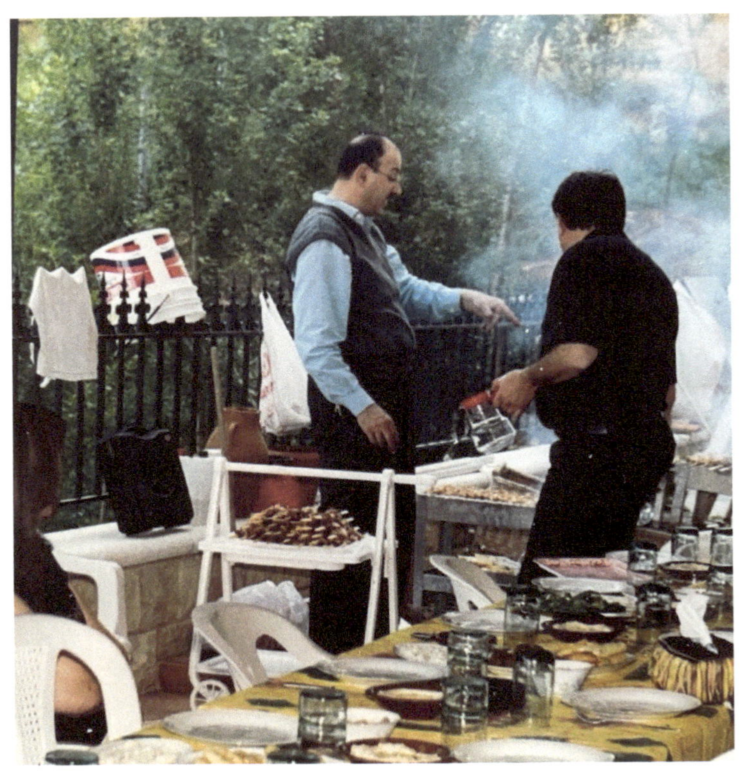

## Terrace Gathering – Lebanon

*On a shaded terrace in Lebanon, smoke curls between friends as conversation stirs the coals. Here, cooking is never solitary — it's a shared act of memory and mastery, where time slows, flavors deepen, and the meal begins long before it's served.*

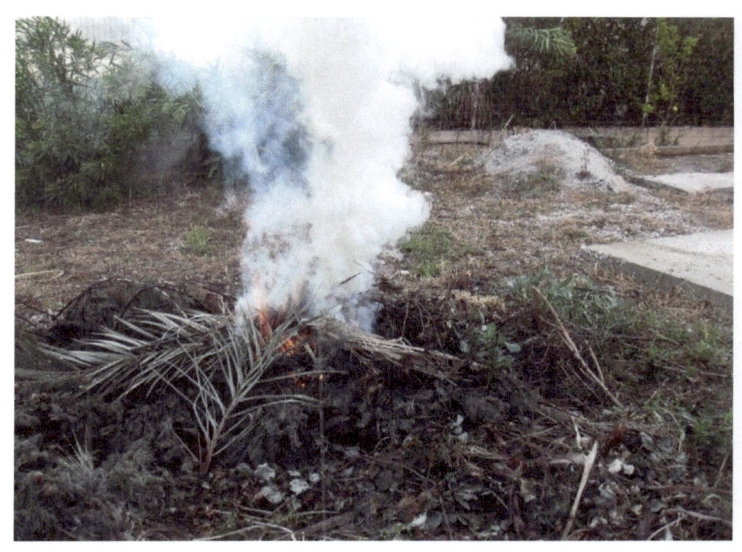

*The fire that transforms flavor also tempers spirit.
When the smoke clears, what remains is essence —
of wood, of labor, of life itself.*

*Photographs courtesy of MILES UP and Eugenia Canaan.*

# Author's Closing Reflections

## Reflecting Back on my own Kitchen Sauces

I've shared some of my sauce foundations in these pages, but don't feel you have to follow them verbatim.

Cooking, like travel, is most rewarding when it takes a few detours. Taste often, trust your instincts, and don't be afraid to make mistakes — they season the craft as much as success does.

After a few tries, you will land on your perfect balance of smoke, spice, and sweetness.

## Looking Ahead

If you've made it this far, you already know that smoke isn't just flavor — it's language.

Every fire you've built, every rack you've tended, every patient hour between too much and just enough... that's where the real craft lives.

When I wrote *Racked & Poured*, I was chasing rhythm — how stories and spirits meet behind the bar. With *The Art of Smoking*, I chased patience — the quiet alchemy between fire and flavor.

The next chapter in this culinary journey is called *From Fire to Flavor: Recipes Across Continents.*
It will gather dishes and ideas that wander from Morocco's spice markets to Sweden's fjord kitchens, from the street grills of Vietnam and Peru to the comfort pots of Ireland and Turkey.

Some of these recipes I learned from fellow chefs in restaurant kitchens, some from friends who taught through laughter and late nights, and others from memories that somehow still smell like garlic and sea air.

*The smoke might fade, but curiosity never does.*

Here's to good company, full plates, and the next story rising from the grill, skillet, or maybe even from an open fire.

**— Alessandro Asante**

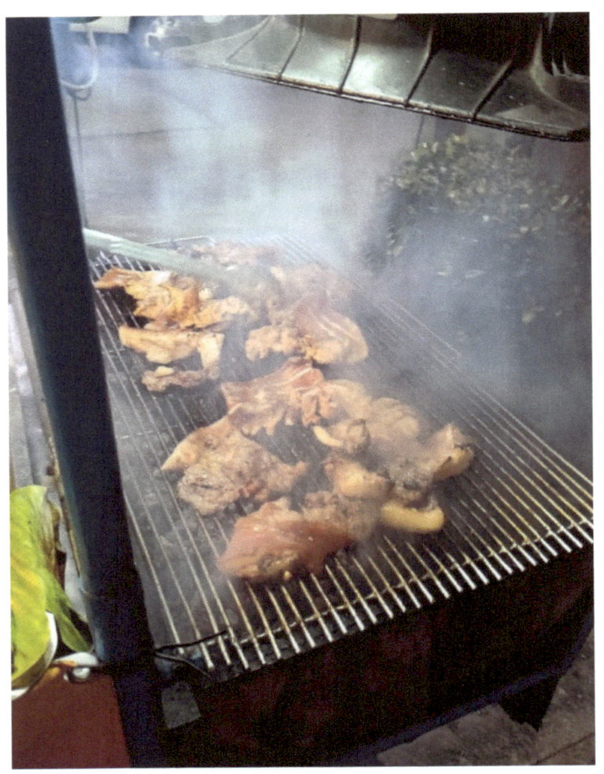

## Back Cover — Closing Reflection

The back cover captures a Thai grill alive with
motion — layers of pork turning slowly through
ribbons of smoke.

As dusk settles, the air thickens with the scent of
flame and time, echoing the morning's first fire from
the street stand on the front cover.

Together, these two moments frame *The Art of
Smoking* — a day's quiet journey from kindled coals
to fading embers, honoring **craft, patience, and the
mastery of fire shared across cultures.**

9 780989 193290